Selected Poems of
FULKE GREVILLE

Edited with an Introduction by
THOM GUNN

FABER AND FABER
24 Russell Square
London

First published in 1968
by Faber and Faber Limited
24 Russell Square London WC1
Printed in Great Britain by
The Bowering Press Plymouth
All rights reserved
SBN 571 08740 x

Contents

Note on the Text

The purpose of this book is to make Greville's short poems available, since the last edition of them has been out of print for some time. In addition to the complete short poems and selected choruses from the plays, I originally intended to include one of Greville's long poems, but I decided against it because two of them are currently in print, and because there are adequate specimens of Greville's didactic style at its best already to be found among the short poems and the choruses (e.g. CII of *Caelica*). My text comes from G. Bullough's edition, *Poems and Dramas of Fulke Greville, First Lord Brooke*, published by Oliver and Boyd in 1939. I have modernized the spelling, but have left the original punctuation untouched, except in a few instances where it seriously impeded a modern reader's understanding. I thank Oliver and Boyd for the permission to use Bullough's text modernized. I have supplied notes to the poems, and as will be seen Bullough's notes have often been of great use to me, though in a few places I have disagreed with them. I also owe thanks to Enid Welsford, for her generosity in lending me her copy of Bullough's edition, to Helena Shire and Tony Tanner for their help and advice, and to Yvor Winters, who some years ago first encouraged me to read Greville. None of these people, of course, are responsible for any errors I have made.

T. G.

Life and Works

There is not a great deal to say about Fulke Greville's life, which was for the most part that of a highly placed civil servant. He was born in 1554 in Warwickshire, where his father was a big landowner. From childhood he and Philip Sidney were close friends: they came to court together, and both prepared for a life of public service in diplomacy, administration, and war. Greville was much valued by the Queen, as may be inferred from her preventing him from going abroad as much as he wanted: more than once, on his way to the continent, he was stopped at ports by her orders and so had to return to court.

Greville shared with Sidney an interest in Calvinism, which was also a political interest in that century when 'religious opinion was, far more often than not, political opinion also.'[1] It is important to remember, though, that their Calvinism was not that brand of Puritan thought which challenged the authority of the monarch.

They also shared a devotion to the art of poetry. Sidney was a kind of sixteenth century Ezra Pound, the most influential poet and critic of his time; and Greville, his closest friend, was obviously the first to be caught up in his experimental excitement: it is likely indeed that they would sometimes write on chosen themes in conscious rivalry.[2] As a result of Sidney's influence, fame, and example, Wilton, the country house of his sister, the Countess of Pembroke, became a centre of patronage. And not only his friends Greville and Dyer, but Spenser, countless sonneteers who never knew him personally, and a whole decade

[1] J. W. Allen, *A History of Political Thought in the Sixteenth Century*, 1928, p. 78.

[2] This is suggested by John Buxton in *Sir Philip Sidney and the English Renaissance*.

of pastoral poets in the 1590's, fed on Sidney's example and were more influenced by him than by any other writer.

Sidney's death in 1586 was the most deeply affecting event in Greville's life. He wanted to go with Leicester into the Low Countries and fight where Sidney had died, but Elizabeth refused to let him, having already lost one valued servant. He resisted her at first, but finally gave way:

'I finding the specious fires of youth to prove far more scorching than glorious, called my second thoughts to counsel, and in that map clearly discerning action and honour, to fly with more wings than one: and that it was sufficient for the plant to grow where his sovereign's hand had placed it; I found reason to contract my thoughts from these larger, but wandering horizons, of the world abroad, and to bound my prospect within the safe limits of duty, in such home services, as were acceptable to my sovereign.'[1]

Thereafter he worked at court for Elizabeth, holding increasingly important positions. He withdrew for a few years on her death, but returned to work for James I and then Charles I. In 1621 he was made Lord Brooke, and by the time of his death had become one of the richest men in the country. In 1628 he was stabbed and killed by an old servant who believed he had not been provided for in his will. Greville himself composed the epitaph which was inscribed on the monument to him in a church in Warwick: 'Servant to Queen Elizabeth, Councillor to King James, Friend to Sir Philip Sidney.'

Except for a few poems from *Caelica* and a pirated edition of one of his plays, none of Greville's writings appeared during his lifetime. As a result, there is no certainty about the dates of his works. However, their order of composition can be conjectured.

Caelica, the collection of his short poems, must come earliest. Bullough believes that the poems were started between 1577 and 1580 and that they were all, or almost all, written by 1600. Moreover he considers that they are arranged in a roughly

[1] Greville, *Life of Sidney*.

chronological order, a belief which is supported by considerations of style and subject matter.

It is perhaps unfortunate that Greville's best-known poem in modern times has been 'O wearisome condition of humanity,' since it is a chorus from one of the plays, and anyone who likes it well enough to read more of him would probably turn first to that play and be rather bored. Greville wrote two plays, *Mustapha* and *Alaham*, though he tells us of another, about Antony and Cleopatra, which he destroyed on the fall of Essex, for fear of misinterpretation. His object in the plays was 'to trace out the high ways of ambitious governors.'[3] They are deliberately closet dramas, in which there is no attempt at character delineation or control of dramatic pace; they are in fact virtually long poems divided into scenes consisting of lengthy rhetorical speeches exchanged by the characters.

We know that the treatises, or long poems, on *Humane Learning, Fame and Honour, Wars, Monarchy*, and *Religion*, followed the plays, growing out of them, since they 'were first intended to be for every act a chorus.'[1] They are often swifter moving than the plays, for Greville is now no longer impeded by what was for him the mere artifice of dramatic convention, but they are extremely uneven in the writing. For stretches they are stylistically merely versified essays, though there are passages of great power alternating with much that is lame and verbose. They do not have the consistent rhetorical power and cunning of Dryden's didactic poems; like Greville's plays, they are of greater historical than literary interest. U. M. Ellis Fermor's is the best comment on them:

'Much of his speculative poetry is an undergrowth of statement, inference, reference and deduction, contradicting and balancing each other, until no conclusion is free from its corresponding doubt, no imaginative experience complete and clear. . . . Through long passages in these poems . . . he seems to lay a generous foundation for his interpretation of human destiny and then, unable to comprehend the elements he has assembled,

<hr />

[1] Greville, *Life of Sidney*.

to go astray among them, to be saved from pedantic frivolity only by a certain weary magnificence of intention persisting in a task beyond its strength.'[1]

Lastly there is the *Life of Sidney*, a long prose work intended as dedication to Greville's collected works that were never published during his lifetime. It is both more and less than a life of his friend, which occupies only the first two-thirds of the work, the remainder being largely a political essay with some interesting autobiographical detail.

[1] U. M. Ellis Fermor, Introduction, *Caelica*. This modernization of *Caelica* appeared as a limited edition brought out by the Greynog Press, Montgomeryshire, in 1939, and I do not believe the useful Introduction has since been reprinted.

Introduction

I

Literary Background

Greville came of age at a time when English poetry was already vigorous, self-conscious, and mature. Rumours to the contrary have no doubt been caused by the literary historians who pay much attention to a popular work like *A Mirror for Magistrates* and little to the contemporary collections of short poems. The first usefully illustrates orthodox Elizabethan political thought but is crudely written and dull; the others tell us comparatively little about such things but sometimes contain poetry of great strength. Predominant among the best poets before Sidney and Greville were Sir Thomas Wyatt, whose poems were not widely circulated until the publication of Tottel's miscellany in 1557, and George Gascoigne, whose poems were published in 1573 and 1575. There was also a large body of impressive anonymous poetry, mainly songs and ballads, which had a direct and clear influence on the later Elizabethans.

The ruling style before Sidney has been called native, plain, and drab, depending on whether the describer has liked or disliked it. Characteristically it is based on statement (rather than metaphor), often compressed into *sententiae*, which were sometimes printed in italics. At its worst, the effect is of plodding metrical prose—the statements are pompously didactic, the *sententiae* are only too easily separable from their contexts, the device of alliteration becomes heavy, and the rhythms are monotonous and unvaried. At its best, it has a compactness in which alliteration becomes a grace like the grace of rhyme, and in which the movement is emphatic without becoming deadening; and the straightforwardness of language and device is the very medium through which energy of thought and feeling emerges. In Gascoigne the style can take on great power. Here is an example where, speaking in the third person, he describes how he gave up trying to be a courtier to become a soldier:

> But now behold what mark the man doth find:
> He shoots to be a soldier in his age;
> Mistrusting all the virtues of the mind,
> He trusts the power of his personage,
> As though long limbs led by a lusty heart
> Might yet suffice to make him rich again;
> But flushing frays have taught him such a part
> That now he thinks the wars yield no such gain.
> And sure I fear, unless your lordship deign,
> To train him yet into some better trade,
> It will be long before he hit the vein,
> Whereby he may a richer man be made.
> He cannot climb as other catchers can,
> To lead a charge before himself be led;
> He cannot spoil the simple sakeless man
> Which is content to feed him with his bread;
> He cannot pinch the painful soldier's pay
> And shear him out his share in ragged sheets;
> He cannot stop to take a greedy prey
> Upon his fellows grovelling in the streets;
> He cannot pull the spoil from such as pill,
> And seem full angry at such foul offense,
> Although the gain content his greedy will
> Under the cloak of contrary pretence.
>
> ('Gascoigne's Woodmanship')

Yvor Winters has distinguished between two kinds of plain style among the Elizabethans—the aphoristic and the expository.[1] Clearly this passage is expository, but its derivation from the aphorism is noticeable: a line like 'He cannot climb as other catchers can' has both the generalizing force and the alliterative

[1] Yvor Winters, 'The 16th Century Lyric in England', *Poetry*, February, March, and April, 1939. This section of my essay owes a good deal to his article.

manner of the aphorism. But it is more than aphorism, in that it cannot be separated from its context. Its succinctness and directness only serve to make clearer the complexity of Gascoigne's attitude to his experience. He cannot help regretting his failure, but at the same time his regret is tempered by his knowledge of the brutality and unscrupulousness of those who 'succeed' as soldiers. The writing contains a good deal of general moral comment, but it is completely saved from mere didacticism by the sensitive fluctuation of the tone from one of vigorous self-criticism to one of unpretentious humanity. Both in the extract and in the poem as a whole the larger implications are constantly related to his personal feelings and actions, and exist only in that relationship.

Gascoigne's remarks about poetry are a great deal more naive than his practice. In his *Certain Notes of Instruction* he speaks of 'invention' as 'the first and most necessary' element of poetry. What he means by invention is made clear from the following passage:

'If I should disclose my pretence in love, I would either make a strange discourse of some intolerable passion, or find occasion to plead by the example of some history, or discover my disquiet in shadows *per Allegoriam*, or use the covertest mean that I could to avoid the uncomely customs of common writers.'

He means something very simple: inventiveness, we would say, or ingenuity, so as to persuade or even trick the reader into accepting what one says by one's attractive indirection. It is remarkable, however, that Gascoigne in practice is direct and muscular, and that there is seldom to be found in his poetry that excess of ornamentation which is the vice often resulting from over-ingenuity. 'Invention' as he actually uses it in his 'Lullaby' or 'Woodmanship' is a mastering or organizing rather than a local or incidental device: in the one he uses the form of a lullaby to sing his youth, his 'gazing eyes', his will, and 'Robin' to sleep; in the other he uses the metaphor of the hunt, where his missing the deer with his arrows symbolizes his past failures, his missing of chances.

[15]

But in his precept of elaboration and indirection, he looks forward to the most famous development in Elizabethan poetry, that initiated by Sidney. Many poets suffered—and continued to suffer, well into the next century—from a puzzled sense of national inferiority to the classical and Italian poets. Sidney enquires in his *Apology* 'why England (the mother of excellent minds) should be grown so hard a stepmother to poets.' Sidney and his friends therefore made a conscious attempt to extend the range of English poetry by exercising it in as many ways as possible, exploring new metres and verse-forms, enlarging its vocabulary, and imitating foreign models. In particular, Sidney was at pains to anglicize the Petrarchan sonnet (which Wyatt had already introduced into the country) in his *Astrophel and Stella*, and the Ariostian epic, of which the *Arcadia* was intended as a prose equivalent. The result of his efforts was an emphasis, in many of his poems and in the poems of writers influenced by him, not only on elaborate mastering devices but also on local inventiveness, which often took the form of ornate imagery.

Without these deliberate attempts at sophistication, such writing as the famous sonnet on the moon would have been almost unthinkable:

With how sad steps, O Moon, thou climb'st the skies!
How silently, and with how wan a face!
What, may it be that even in heavenly place
That busy archer his sharp arrows tries?
Sure, if that long-with-love-acquainted eyes
Can judge of love, thou feel'st a lover's case:
I read it in thy looks: thy languish'd grace,
To me that feel the like, thy state descries.
Then even of fellowship, O Moon, tell me,
Is constant love deem'd there but want of wit?
Are beauties there as proud as here they be?
Do they above love to be lov'd, and yet
Those lovers scorn whom that love doth possess?
Do they call virtue there ungratefulness?

(Astrophel and Stella, **XXXI**)

[16]

It starts with the halting regretful movement of Sidney's perception (the first line would have a different effect if it read 'O Moon, with how sad steps thou climb'st the skies'), and then quickens slightly as he forms the conceit of the third and fourth lines. The resemblance between the moon and the lover is a good deal more tenuous than the resemblance Gascoigne found between missing deer and missing chances, for Sidney's comparison depends entirely on the fact that the moon is slow in its movement, and therefore seems sad, like a sad lover. Yet once this resemblance is granted it works surely and aptly, since Sidney uses it tactfully and never presses it into absurdity: the earthly lover is compared to those 'above' or 'there' rather than to the moon itself, and thus we are not tempted to take the comparison so literally that we ask awkward questions like 'Who is the moon in love with?' Moreover the verse movement continues to be fully alive at every point, and the four questions at the end are delivered with all the variety of rhetoric at Sidney's command, rising to the impatience of the third in which the speaker is so obsessed with love that he uses the word four times in two lines, and sinking to the more desperate tone of the simpler and more personally felt last line.

On the other hand, though the new kind of elaboration is in this poem magnificently justified, such a poem as *Astrophel and Stella* XCIX shows the vices of an overdependence on ornament, ornament here that does not inform the poem as a whole but is strictly local, and is not even doing its local job well. The lover describes how he lies awake, 'viewing the shape of darkness,' in the first eight lines, which are clear and strong. The sonnet ends:

> But when birds charm and that sweet air which is
> Morn's messenger with rose-enamell'd skies
> Calls each wight to salute the flower of bliss,
> In tombs of lids then buried are mine eyes,
> Forc'd by their lord, who is asham'd to find
> Such light in sense with such a darken'd mind.

A simple thought is here being dressed up in clothes of a rather tawdry richness. Clearly there were losses as well as gains in having advanced beyond the plain style. Not only are the words imprecisely and tritely decorative (charm, sweet, rose-enamell'd), but there is a tendency to ridiculous circumlocution, as in the fourth line quoted, and Sidney is led into damaging vagueness in at least two phrases suggesting deliquescent conceits: we shall never know exactly what the flower of bliss may be, and is the lord of the eyes merely Sidney himself, or his mind, or someone not mentioned in the poem—the god of love, perhaps?

There were thus two styles available—the plain and the ornate. There was to be, of course, a third stage of elaboration, in the metaphysical image. It was already latent in the Petrarchan conceit: given the conceit, and given the interest in ingenuity, it was inevitable. One of the fascinating things about reading Shakespeare's sonnets and early plays is to find him often hovering in that area between the conceit and the metaphysical image where a figure is so far elaborated that it is no longer simply the one but not so far elaborated that it can be called the other. Certainly the metaphysical image would have emerged without Donne, and it is possible that it did emerge before him, but it was left to Donne to develop it with such ruthless consistency that at times he appears to be parodying the device while at others he uses it with a strength that no one else equalled.

Such a categorization as I have just attempted is not original, it is a commonplace of literary history. Nor is it complete, as a description of the styles available to Elizabethans. And in one way it is confusing for the modern reader, for we tend, nowadays, to think of literary 'schools' as mutually exclusive: we know, for example, that William Carlos Williams wrote much of his best poetry during the last fifteen years of Thomas Hardy's life, but he never wrote like Hardy, nor did Hardy ever write like Williams. John Hollander has said, 'For a true poet, we feel today, all occasions, subjects, forms and conventions must come under the absolute command of one governing style,' and he goes on to point out that no such feeling obtained with the Elizabethans.[1] The earlier plain style continued to be available, and some of the best poetry of Sidney, Shakespeare, Jonson, and

[1] John Hollander, Introduction, *Ben Jonson*, Laurel Poetry Series, 1961, p. 13.

[18]

Donne is written in it. Thomas Churchyard, one of the most plodding poets of the plain style, was made welcome at Wilton, from which the 'New Poetry' had emerged. He was evidently considered a senior poet worthy of respect whose style had not been rejected. And we find a good many poets between 1575 and 1600 who wrote in the plain style and in the Petrarchan and even in the metaphysical as well. Ralegh is one who can be taken as a kind of epitome of Elizabethan poetry, moving through the different styles and never relinquishing what he learned from each. Another is Greville.

II

CAELICA: Early Poems

If the poems in *Caelica* are in chronological order, as is likely, then we notice that at certain times the dominant Elizabethan styles co-exist in Greville's work, though he starts by being most interested in the Petrarchan experiment, and though in the later poems he deliberately changes to a plain style. Of course, there is variety not only in what he is attempting but in the success of the attempts: of the hundred and nine poems in the collection there are several outright failures, several stiff pieces of writing similar to the dullest parts of the *Treatises*, and several formulary sonnets that never get beyond their formulae. But we re-read a poet for his best poems, and with Greville as with many other poets it is interesting to read his failures, since they help us better to understand his successes.

In the earliest of the love poems alone, we are already confronted by an extraordinary richness and diversity. Some of them recall to me poems, probably written later, by other poets. To speak of these resemblances is not to display my own perspicuity, nor is it to suggest that others looted Greville's manuscripts. It is to suggest the persistence of certain traditions. Nowadays the journalistic critical cliché about a young poet is to say that 'he has found his own voice,' the emphasis being on his differentness, on

[19]

the uniqueness of his voice, on the fact that he sounds like nobody else. But the Elizabethans at their best as well as at their worst are always sounding like each other. They did not search much after uniqueness of voice: what Gascoigne was perfecting, what Sidney was exploring, were usable styles in which the individual could have the freedom to do the most he was capable of, styles which could be inherited by and shared with others who had the talent. It would hardly have struck them that a style could be used for display of personality. So it is not surprising that we notice resemblances to more famous poems in this early work of Greville's. There is the eloquence of 'The world, that all contains, is ever moving' (VII), an extended sonnet and one of the best examples of that Elizabethan kind (of which Shakespeare's 'When to the sessions of sweet silent thought' is another) in which the mutability of the world is considered by the poet, and then is abruptly contradicted by the contemplation of the loved one, who has the permanence of a Platonic Form. In a poem like 'Why how now Cupid, do you covet change?', a sonnet very far from the rather frigid sonnet-exercises that are also present in *Caelica*, ingenuity of thought combines with a conversational directness rather similar to what we sometimes find in Drayton and Donne. And in 'I, with whose colours Myra dress'd her head' (XXII), the pastoral simplesse and mellifluous loveliness of line suggest the better-known but later songs of Lodge and Greene—almost, but not quite, over-pretty.

> I, that on Sunday at the church-stile found
> A garland sweet, with true-love-knots in flowers,
> Which I to wear about mine arm was bound,
> That each of us might know that all was ours:
> > Must I now lead an idle life in wishes?
> > And follow Cupid for his loaves, and fishes?

Of the last line, Bullough comments 'he does not want to be merely one among five thousand, dependent on miracles for his sustenance.'[1] For Cupid is the Christ of the religion of love. And

[1] G. Bullough, note in *Poems and Dramas of Fulke Greville, Lord Brooke*, 1939, vol. 1, p. 241.

on a closer inspection it is not hard to see how far this pastoral is from a real country song. Rather, it is in that Elizabethan convention in which the already anglicized secular Mariolatory of the troubadours rejoins its later development Petracrhanism (a double tradition to become so overworked by the 1590's that it would be ribaldly parodied by Shakespeare and Donne). In Greville's early poetry we find the lover as acolyte or worshipper in that religion where Cupid takes the place of Christ and the mistress the place of either Mary or God. She is moreover a cruel mistress—she is desired sexually and she rejects him sexually, and perhaps rejects him outright. To complicate matters, the whole is often conceived in a pastoral setting of great formality, the formality of which we may not recognize at once, since often there are also present echoes of real folk songs (as in the line 'Fools only hedge the cuckoo in,' from LII). Such religious-pastoral metaphors were becoming commonplaces, but when Greville and Sidney first used them they were still metaphors with potential, neither meaningless nor meaningful in themselves.

What Greville was able to do within the tradition which he was helping to define is seen very interestingly in X, not a pastoral but fully Petrarchan. It is neither so inventive nor so attractive as the poems I have just mentioned, but it is worth while examining closely, since it shows him exploring the methods and metaphors in a clean and workmanlike manner: and it is a kind of starting point which is already full of hints of later directions. This is the first stanza:

> Love, of man's wandering thoughts the restless being,
> Thou from my mind with glory wast invited,
> Glory of those fair eyes, where all eyes, seeing
> Virtue's and beauty's riches, are delighted;
> What angel's pride, or what self-disagreeing,
> What dazzling brightness hath your beams benighted,
> > That fallen thus from those joys which you aspired,
> > Down to my darken'd mind you are retired?

Love, we see, is practically an allegorical quality, since it existed before the mistress invited it out of Greville's mind, and the first line suggests that it existed even before it had an object. It becomes like an angel, specifically Lucifer. The mistress is Godlike in her dazzling brightness, and Love falls, back into Greville's mind, which therefore becomes Hell. The writing of the stanza is formal and rhetorical without being grandiloquent; fluent and clean but barely holding itself this side of cliché: the first line and later the word 'self-disagreeing' are so far all there is to reassure us that we have not read this poem before. At the same time, the hyperbolic metaphor is handled with exceptional care: for Greville at this point suggests, he does not yet quite state, that God, Lucifer, and Hell are in the poem.

But in the second stanza, the lover's mind bears all the marks of Hell:

> Within which mind since you from thence ascended,
> Truth clouds itself, wit serves but to resemble,
> Envy is king, at others' good offended,
> Memory doth worlds of wretchedness assemble,
> Passion to ruin passion is intended,
> My reason is but power to dissemble;
>   Then tell me Love, what glory you divine
>   Yourself can find within this soul of mine?

Here the formality of demeanour remains constant, but the type of perception emerging from the conceit of the fallen angel shows the peculiar direction Greville was already able to give to the convention. 'Memory doth worlds of wretchedness assemble.' The line has the Elizabethan fullness that we find in certain other lines of Greville's (the adequacy and beauty of, for example, 'A simple goodness in the flesh refin'd' or, speaking about children, 'They cry to have, and cry to cast away'). The language of the line is general, but it is a different kind of generality from that of the first stanza, where he was picking his way between certain risks of taste: the generality here is a summation of experience and not an evasion of it. 'Assemble', seeming in the first instant a neutral and innocuous word, in the next is seen as shockingly accurate: this is what memory does do in a period of unhappiness, it deliberately and carefully and painstakingly reconstructs the

[22]

past causes of present misery, with the perverse result that the accuracy and completeness of its reconstruction only increases the misery. Love, we see, is something so vital that when it is unshared, when it is in exile and has no willingly accepting object, it creates confusion and conflict by its very vitality, and becomes a kind of malignancy. The mind to which Love is exiled is dominated by frustration and deprived of the mistress, like Lucifer in Hell, who is dominated by desires for his past state and deprived of God. But unlike Lucifer, this fallen angel is given a second chance, which is described in the last stanza:

> Rather go back unto that heavenly choir
> Of Nature's riches, in her beauties placed,
> And there in contemplation feed desire,
> Which till it wonder, is not rightly graced;
> For those sweet glories, which you do aspire,
> Must as ideas only be embraced,
>   Since excellence in other form enjoyed,
>   Is by descending to her saints destroyed.

He is allowed to try again, he may return. He must cease desiring her physically but he may embrace her as an idea, or rather as the Idea, the Form of forms, a secular absolute. The last stanza returns us to the manner of the first. We have had a short glimpse of things as we know they are, and we go back now to a theoretical and formulary love, such as can only exist on paper. The Platonic-Petrarchan commonplaces are conveyed with tact and carefulness of language that does not allow the hyperboles to become ridiculous. But the poem is more than an exercise. It succeeds because the commonplaces are darkened, in the middle stanza, with an accuracy of feeling which takes us far beyond the mere conceit, and thus by juxtaposition gives the formulary bits a validity they would not otherwise have.

Deprivation and despair are themes probably no more common in Greville's than in most people's love poems, but he makes them his peculiar province, even as early as this, by the intensity of his apprehension of them. And as we go through *Caelica* we notice more and more how these intensely-apprehended themes are the characteristic of Greville's handling of the love-conventions.

III

CAELICA: Middle Poems

A poem like XLV treats of an associated subject, absence, but very differently. The cause of deprivation in X appeared to be rejection, or conditional rejection, by the mistress; but in XLV the deprivation is caused simply by a geographical separation for a certain time. The tone of much of the poem is witty and sceptical: addressing Absence, Greville says,

> When bankrupt Cupid braveth,
> Thy mines his credit saveth,
> With sweet delays.

The paradox is that absence enables the lover to live up to his protestations by increasing his love, because absence makes the heart grow fonder. But the tone of the careful courtier is preserved at the same time. Lest such lines seem too uncomplimentary, however true they may be, they are balanced by the delicate flattery of:

> Absence, like dainty clouds,
> On glorious bright,
> Nature weak senses shrouds
> From harming light.

That is, absence shields his eyes from her dazzling light, which he is too weak to contemplate for long. Her light is no longer that of God, but in this poem merely that of the sun. Then the series of conceits praising Absence turns, logically enough, into a derogation of Presence. In the mistress' presence he desires her sexually; but, he goes on, continuing the metaphor of light,

> Absence is free:
> Thoughts do in absence venter
> On Cupid's shadow'd centre,
> They wink and see.

With the naming of 'Cupid's shadow'd centre,' referring back not only to the 'dainty clouds' of the earlier image but to the darkness of his lust, the tone itself becomes shadowed by the fact that they are separated, and the desire to swallow incompleteness of experience in the completions of epigrammatic conceits is slackened. Memory doth worlds of wretchedness assemble.

> But thoughts be not so brave
> With absent joy;
> For you with that you have
> Your self destroy.
> The absence which you glory
> Is that which makes you sorry
> And burn in vain;
> For thought is not the weapon
> Wherewith thought's ease men cheapen
> Absence is pain.

Thought of her, after all, is not the means by which he can cheaply obtain 'thought's ease'. Each stanza has ended with a line of two feet, and the poem must end with such a line also. But the last line here is more abruptly separated from the preceding statement than are the last lines in the previous stanzas, and it differs from them also in consisting of a trochee and an iamb rather than of two iambs, so giving the line an additional separating emphasis. It is a slight device, but one which has a considerable effect, for a small change in the context of regular repetition has the effect of a big change in an irregular context. It is set apart, abrupt, even though the statements before it lead up to it logically enough. Absence *is* pain, after all, and the ingenuity of one's conceits is merely a concealment of real feeling.

But the act of concealment is also a proof of there being something to conceal. In light of the ending, the ingenuity of the conceits can be seen not as mere trifling but as psychologically functional in the poem. One does try to smile things out, to joke about them, until the smiles and jokes begin to cut too deeply into the emotions they are covering. And one of the marks of

Greville's love poems is the penetration and accuracy with which they describe the perversity of human emotions. Bullough points out the frequency, throughout Greville's poetry, of compounds prefixed 'self'. In X, it was when love was imprisoned in the underworld of the self that it got infected. And in states of deprivation one is left with merely the elements of the self warring together, for the self is part of fallen Nature, and can only become refined with assistance from outside—from God, that is, or from the lady (who is a God-substitute).

The implications of self-defeat are fully explored in LVI, 'All my senses, like beacon's flame,' a poem about sexual action not taken. In theme it is very similar to Sidney's great sonnet 'I might, unhappy word, ah me, I might.' Each is one of the best poems its author wrote, and yet there is a world of contrast in their treatment of their common theme. Sidney uses largely plain speech in his poem, allowing a very dramatic verse movement to do much of the work in conveying the bursts and hesitations of his emotion, while Greville is ornate in his imagery and elaborate in his strategy. In the last poem discussed he had clearly mastered the 'conceited' love convention, but here he projects it so far from its beginnings that if the poem were anonymous we would swear that it was written in the mid-seventeenth century rather than at the end of the sixteenth.

The poem is in seven-syllable tetrameter lines, a difficult metre that tends to stiffness because of the rather heavy emphasis given to the first syllable of the line. But it is used here with great flexibility; and it is particularly brisk at the start, where the lover himself is brisk, determined to seduce Cynthia. Her name should already give us a clue to the outcome of the poem, for Cynthia is chastity herself and cannot be seduced, but the lover does not realize this. He is a lusty young warrior, confident and vigorous —and rash, as it turns out. He goes to her, and apparently finds her asleep, naked. Under the night sky he is led into a kind of vision of the gods, among whom he finds himself. Yet his is a false confidence. He becomes the child of his fantasy and loses his chance. (It is not at once clear what has happened in the literal situation, but later in line 35 we gather that she has been 'unkind', and finally in lines 45–8 that he has delayed when he could have taken her.)

> I stepp'd forth to touch the sky,
> I a god by Cupid dreams;
> Cynthia who did naked lie,
> Runs away like silver streams,
> Leaving hollow banks behind,
> Who can neither forward move,
> Nor if rivers be unkind
> Turn away or leave to love.

The imagery thus far in the poem has been continuously linked; but the transition in the fourth line quoted is almost surrealistic, where the moonlight becomes water draining away. For she is pure light—not that of God, or even the sun this time, but the light, silvery, of the moon. He is left standing by the dried river bed, on the banks and also *like* them, for banks normally clasp the stream but here they clasp nothing. 'There stand I' he goes on— and fairly deliberately there is a sexual metaphor implied.

> There stand I, like Arctic Pole,
> Where Sol passeth o'er the line,
> Mourning my benighted soul,
> Which so loseth light divine.

He has lost all light now. Even water is inaccessible, being turned to ice. He stands desperate, isolated, and sterile, like the Pole, which Greville seems to visualize as something actually pole-like, or maybe even as a kind of mountain. Then there is a transition.

> There stand I like men that preach
> From the execution place,
> At their death content to teach
> All the world with their disgrace.

The lonely figure and its background melt surreally, for the last time, into a similar constant figure against another background. Now he is doomed, he is a living example of what not to do or

[27]

be. The image of the man making his speech from the scaffold leads easily to the concluding lines (which constitute that speech) on a traditional theme fully brought to life by delicate rueful ironies. He dies because *she* did not 'die'—in the second sense, of sexual orgasm, that the Elizabethans were endlessly fond of giving to the word. The condemned man's advice to lovers is to waste no time in dreaming or in idealizing: for love is 'Nature's art', it is earthly or it is nothing. The poem ends,

> None can well behold with eyes
> But what underneath him lies.

While he was a god in the heaven of his imagination, the real Cynthia was still on earth. Moreover, the ideal is 'above' man, while sex is 'beneath' him, a lower sort of activity. And Cynthia lying there as he stands by her bed is also physically beneath him. The resemblance to Marvell here becomes uncanny: it was already there in the fantasy and ingenuity of the transformations —each image clear and hard in itself but melting easily, though surprisingly, into the next; it was there in the mixture of lyricism and irony bathing the whole poem; it is here most of all in the complexity of meaning in the last two lines. It is as good a poem as the best of Marvell's, and for something like the reasons that Marvell is good: it is the result of a confrontation between, on the one hand, an awareness of the grace and delicacy of courtly love at its best, and, on the other, an equally full awareness of the way things are in life itself, where such idealism is simply irrelevant.

I have so far disregarded those numerous poems in which Greville uses a style largely free of imagery. They are an important part even of his early work, but they are not the whole of Greville. His earlier intention seems to have been to explore the ornate conventions to their utmost, and he certainly carried them to their extreme in the metaphysical imagery of LXVIII ('While that my heart an altar I did make') and of LXI ('Caelica, while you do swear that you do love me best'). (The latter at one point even topples into the slightly ludicrous effects that such imagery always risks:

[28]

> The leaves fall off, when sap goes to the root,
> The warmth doth clothe the bough again;
> And to the dead tree what doth boot,
> The silly man's manuring pain?)

It is not true that Greville seems ill at ease in the ornate poems, as has sometimes been implied. He mastered the Petrarchan convention, and experimented widely and successfully in a number of styles, from the 'artless' pastoralism of XXII or LII to the high sophistication and rather troubled elaboration of the poem just discussed. In these poems alone he stands with the best of the Elizabethans and early Jacobeans, because his ingenuity seldom escapes from the facts of the world: absence, after all, is pain; love is only Nature's art—and his regret at such facts is expressed cleanly, artfully, and movingly.

IV

Nature and the Need for Authority

After the love poems there is a short miscellaneous group, which is followed by a pair of sonnets, LXXXIV and LXXXV, the one a farewell to love, and the other a definition of Christian love which also serves as introduction to the final group of poems. The farewell to love is something of a convention in Elizabethan sonnet sequences, and though *Caelica* is not actually such a sequence it had probably been intended as one at some time or other. But to say it is a convention explains nothing: everything depends on why an author picks a particular convention and on what he does with it. I want to show how this farewell to love and the poem following it are inevitable for Greville given the maturing of his attitudes. Earthly love had to be rejected, sooner or later, because the older one becomes the more clearly one sees through the Platonic rubbish of a poem like X; and if one sees through that then one is left with a love that is 'only Nature's art', a relationship with another human being which even if lasting and meaningful must take place within Nature, and must be subject to her laws. And Nature, for a Christian of the Renaissance, is flawed.

There is much that is difficult to grasp about Greville's views, particularly those he holds about Nature. Perhaps, as G. A. Wilkes has suggested, we find his attitudes so self-contradictory because we are ignorant of the exact chronology of the writings.[1] This may be so, but we are still left with the apparently deliberate juxtaposition of the two final choruses of *Mustapha* (to be found on pp. 148 and 149). U. M. Ellis Fermor says of them:

'In the first chorus he takes the Lucretian "Nature" as the symbol of a beneficent controlling power, but in the second, he reverses Lucretius's conclusion, sees Nature herself as the source of evil and comes, simultaneously, very near to equating this 'Nature' with God. . . . He first condemns superstition and commits man to natural law and then, in a further reach of destructive thought, condemns that natural law itself.'[2]

In *Caelica*, though he has not yet brought his thought to such extreme opposed positions, he already sees Nature as by turns attractive and repulsive. Nevertheless, it does seem possible to sort out his attitudes on the subject as they appear in *Caelica*, even if the sorting out may result in something of an over-simplification. Nature is attractive, and moreover we are born into it, but there are two things wrong with it: first, it is a rival to God in attracting our worship; secondly, it is fallen, along with man, and so is mutable.

It is a rival to God, although created by him, in that man may love the particulars of Nature as an end in themselves. In XCVI 'the wealth of Nature' is seen as a temptation and an obstacle. Nature is the 'fair usurper',

> Yet rules she none, but such as will obey,
> And to that end becomes what they aspire.

[1] G. A. Wilkes, 'The Sequence of Writings of Fulke Greville, Lord Brooke' *Studies in Philology*, vol. LVI, pp. 489–503.
[2] U. M. Ellis Fermor, Introduction, *Caelica*.

And in CII he even considers what would happen if there were no God:

> But grant that there were no eternity,
> That life were all, and pleasure life of it,
> In sin's excess there yet confusions be,
> Which spoil his peace, and passionate his wit,
>   Making his nature less, his reason thrall,
>   To tyranny of vice unnatural.
>
> And as hell-fires, not wanting heat, want light;
> So these strange witchcrafts, which like pleasure be,
> Not wanting fair enticements, want delight,
> Inward being nothing but deformity;
>   But do at open doors let frail powers in
>   To that strait building, Little Ease of sin.

For, as part of fallen Nature, we contain our own confusions. The possibility of a hell in the human mind anticipating the Hell after death is a constant theme of Greville's. Another theme, an almost universal preoccupation of medieval and Elizabethan writers, is that of the mutability of all Nature. Nature is not only fallen, she is finite, subject to time and thus to change. In the third chorus of *Mustapha*, both Time and Eternity say, accurately, 'I am the measure of felicity.' But the two felicities are of a different sort. For Time's 'essence only is to write, and blot.' If you put your trust in the temporal and the finite, you are putting your trust in what will inevitably fail you.

The last observation was not new, nor was it confined to Elizabethans. Similarly Camus called life in a temporal world without sanction 'absurd', but Camus did not discover this fact: he merely put more abruptly what many men have noticed. Interestingly enough, Camus also used the image of Little Ease (*le malconfort*), the cell where one cannot stand, sit, or lie, for the state of a man constrained by a sense of guilt in a world where there is no god and thus where there can be no redemption for that guilt.

[31]

'Il fallait vivre dans le malconfort. . . . Tous les jours,
par l'immuable contrainte qui ankylosait son corps,
le condamné apprenait qu'il était coupable et que
l'innocence consiste à s'étirer joyeusement.'[1]

What is important is not so much the perception of absurdity,
which to a certain kind of thinker is inevitable,[2] as how one
conducts oneself after making that perception. Camus' great
contribution is less in the analysis of the sickness into which we
are born than in the determination to live with that sickness, fully
acknowledging it and accepting it as the basis for our actions.
Greville could not make such an acceptance.

He was supersensitive to the dangers of attempting to stand
on one's own. Thus the crying need for authority, which, by the
time of *Humane Learning*, can lead him into the peculiarly repel-
lent position of advocating terror as a political expedient in the
unified authoritarian state.[3] Those who have a constant sense of
human depravity, like the late Police Chief Parker of Los
Angeles, end up by being able to trust only in the abstraction of
authoritarianism. And Greville, though he varies in his attitude
to political authoritarianism (aware as he is of the fallibility of
princes), is constant in putting ultimate trust only in the Divine
ideal.

It would be a mistake to say that Greville's set of attitudes
were forced on him by his time alone. There were other schools
of thought available—there was, for example, a strong move-
ment by the end of the sixteenth century for an almost complete

---

[1] Albert Camus, *La Chute*, 1956, pp. 126–7.

[2] To a certain kind of thinker in the West, that is. But there have also been
those, from the Cathars to the pantheists and the modern heirs of the pantheists,
who have viewed the world as a place where paradise can be recreated by the re-
jection of all intellectual process.

[3] Greville, *Treatie of Humane Learning*, stanza 92. He is speaking of secular
laws:

> Therefore, as shadows of those laws divine,
> They must assist Church-censure, punish error,
> Since when, from order, nature would decline,
> There is no other native cure but terror;
>   By discipline, to keep the doctrine free,
>   That Faith and Power still relatives may be.

[32]

religious toleration; but Greville was more interested in Calvin's thought with its emphasis on unity and authority. On earth he could be certain only of the weakness, mutability, and uncertainty of all that surround him; and this conviction is very clear in some of the religious poems where he tries to surrender himself to God, and succeeds in that surrender only with a desperation of voice very similar to that of Donne in the Divine Poems.

How one should live the temporal life, ultimately, is by hardly living at all. Those who will reach Heaven, the elect, are described thus in the prologue to *Alaham*:

> Those angel-souls in flesh imprisoned,
> Like strangers living in mortality,
> Still more, and more, themselves inspirited,
> Refining Nature to eternity,
> By being maids in earth's adulterous bed.

The rigour of such a belief gives additional force to such lines as 'The flesh is dead, before grace can be born' (LXXXIX), or 'For God comes not, till man be overthrown;/Peace is the seed of grace, in dead flesh sown' (XCVI). They may be Pauline commonplaces, but they are intended very literally and very passionately by Greville. Practically any value in life is denied except as a preparation for death.

The rejection of life's secular particulars changes not only the subject matter of *Caelica* but the style. Such particulars are evil because they divert man from the abstraction toward which he should be labouring to elevate himself; earth is an adulterous bed, and thus in abandoning the ornate style, which is loaded with the lushness of the finite, Greville is rejecting its inducements stylistically as well.

It is not only a rejection, of course, it is also an acceptance.

> Love is the peace, whereto all thoughts do strive,
> Done and begun with all our powers in one:
> The first and last in us that is alive,
> End of the good, and therewith pleas'd alone.

Perfection's spirit, goddess of the mind,
Passed through hope, desire, grief and fear,
A simple goodness in the flesh refin'd,
Which of the joys to come doth witness bear.

Constant, because it sees no cause to vary,
A quintessence of passions overthrown,
Rais'd above all that change of objects carry,
A nature by no other nature known:
    For glory's of eternity a frame,
    That by all bodies else obscures her name.

Our love for God is both a way to the absolute, and—being an image or imitation of God's love—is in another sense already of the absolute, the end itself. The poem is a beautiful piece of Protestant literature; and the line 'A simple goodness in the flesh refin'd' is a beautiful expression of the Protestant ideal. 'Refine' is one of Greville's favourite words, and it is surely an important word for an understanding of the relation between the particulars of the life the Christian leads and the absolute beyond it. But it is also a useful word to describe what Greville is now attempting to do with his style: for the language itself is being 'refined' of the heavy impurities of the life of this world. The poem, almost void of imagery, gentle and firm in tone, complex in thought but lucid in syntax and language (one cannot always say this of Greville), is one of the triumphs of the plain style, and introduces a section of Greville's poems full of such triumphs.

V

CAELICA: Late Poems

The preceding outline ends as a description of attitudes that I find at best sterile and at worst obnoxious. Of course one has to have a historical sense when discussing ideas of the past. Certain needs at a certain time in history, certain insensitivities which may have counterparts in different but equally extreme modern insensitivities, may account for and on occasion excuse ideas of the past which one finds repugnant. But a poem must be more than the ideas it contains. If it cannot validate itself without one's having to make historical allowances, then it is not likely to be very good. And the poem just quoted does validate the ideas that I had summarized. It puts them in terms of the imagination and makes humane what I would have otherwise called inhumane attitudes: it makes the higher good convincing; and in it love is not the necessity of siding with an authoritarian God but an attempt to capture, and be part of, the rhythm of a divinely created universe.

In many of the following poems a similar validation occurs. In them Greville has moved, as Donne was to do a little later, from the paradoxes of love to the paradoxes of Christianity. The move was an obvious one, given their decision to put away what they considered childish things. The metaphors of worship used in courtly love were originally a translation from the terms of Christian worship, and so now it was a matter of translating them back. Deprivation of the unkind or absent mistress becomes deprivation of God's grace. The mistress had been an absolute, an ideal, an unchangeable, as contrasted to the flawed, fallen, and changeable particulars of creation: so is God.

Most of these poems are written more straightforwardly than those earlier in *Caelica*, and their tone is more consistently serious. God is not to be trifled with, or subjected to ambiguities. The craving for certainty of grace is painful. The *intermittences du coeur* which had provoked, before, a witty shrug, a rueful attempt to joke it out, a depression of the spirits, become now the cause for unqualified lamentation. The change was deliberate and conscious. Greville says in the *Life of Sidney*:

'For my own part, I found my creeping genius more fixed upon the images of life, than the images of wit, and therefore chose not to write to them on whose foot the black ox had not already trod, as the proverb is, but to those only, that are weather-beaten in the sea of this world, such as having lost the sight of

[35]

their gardens and groves, study to sail on a right course among rocks and quicksands.'

When he speaks about 'images of life', Greville is not suggesting the adoption of some kind of sixteenth-century Imagism, he means something like 'reality'. And for him reality had increasingly become a religious matter.

One of the most impressive of these poems is C, on night, which at first sight seems a little out of place among the religious poems. It could be read as a description, simply, of certain common psychological weaknesses. But to do so would be to only partially read it.

> In night when colours all to black are cast,
> Distinction lost, or gone down with the light;
> The eye a watch to inward senses plac'd,
> Not seeing, yet still having power of sight,
>
> Gives vain alarums to the inward sense,
> Where fear stirr'd up with witty tyranny,
> Confounds all powers, and thorough self-offence,
> Doth forge and raise impossibility:
>
> Such as in thick depriving darknesses,
> Proper reflections of the error be,
> And images of self-confusednesses,
> Which hurt imaginations only see;
> And from this nothing seen, tells news of devils,
> Which but expressions be of inward evils.

The first four lines consist of a careful, concise, and accurate description of nightfall and its effect on a man. The observing intelligence is already making itself felt, even in the internal commas of the second and fourth lines, making careful distinctions even about that state in which distinction is lost. It emerges more openly in the second quatrain, in which it both describes and explains. 'Witty tyranny' is the tyranny of wit, or the mind, *on its own*, without outside assistance. One's delusions in darkness, one's 'self-offence', similarly, are the result of a simple dependence on the self rather than on the external, which could act as check and guide: in daylight one can at least depend on external fact (Nature) in order to keep one's sense of proportion. In the ninth line, the state of mind is compared explicitly with the 'thick depriving darknesses' of Hell, where the images (devils, perhaps) are moral error's own reflections. For Elizabethan mirrors reflect in an exemplary fashion, and show here the essence of what is. Superficially it seems a thoroughly rationalistic poem explaining delusion in an almost Freudian way as the result of 'hurt imagination' and 'inward evils', as repression emerging in dream or hallucination, but the whole emphasis of the poem (one should not even need the context of *Caelica*) is on the real Hell, of which the night is simply image, and on the authority, that of God, of which one is deprived.

The previous poem, 'Down in the depth of mine iniquity,' treats of the deprivation of God more directly. In this part of *Caelica* Greville is much preoccupied with the genuineness of prayer. Too often we pray

> Thinking a wish may wear out vanity,
> Or habits be by miracles defac'd.

This poem is not a prayer but a meditation; nevertheless the feeling behind it is similar to that of a man praying: it is governed by the same moral bracing, by the effort to see things as they really are, by the Protestant concern with sincerity. Most of the lines end with the double rhymes Greville is so fond of, and here they help to convey the difficulty, the lack of ease, the strain it imposes on a man to meditate honestly on such a subject and to work his way through to its conclusion.

> Down in the depth of mine iniquity,
> That ugly centre of infernal spirits;
> Where each sin feels her own deformity,
> In those peculiar torments she inherits,
>   Depriv'd of human graces, and divine,
>   Even there appears this saving God of mine.

For comparison and contrast we can think back to the tenth poem: it is almost as though the most important part of Greville's poetry consisted of an attempt to chart the map of Hell. The later poem starts with a description of the state of sin, all the more terrifying for the lack of melodramatic demons: for the Hell here, like that of the poem on night, is caused by deprivation alone. The sinner is in Little Ease, unable to achieve the simple relief of stretching his limbs. Deprivation causes the self to become malignant, and to inherit that torment to which divine grace is an immunization, the torment in which sin recognizes its 'deformity' and can do nothing to change it. The refrain, however, contains a surprise, and flatly juxtaposes the 'saving God'. Nothing in the stanza has prepared us for this: the apprehension of God's grace, at this point of the poem, is something totally illogical, blind faith.

> And in this fatal mirror of transgression,
> Shows man as fruit of his degeneration,
> The error's ugly infinite impression,
> Which bears the faithless down to desperation;
>> Depriv'd of human graces and divine,
>> Even there appears this saving God of mine.

The mirror is again exemplary, but the example here is of God himself (who is in CIX, also, the 'mirror of transgression'). The error, reflected in God, shows up in all its implications: man is degenerate, and fallen, and there is little he can do about it. The vowel-alliteration of the third line makes it easy to say quickly; the error's 'impression' spreads, similarly, with the ease and speed of a stain on water. The despair is absolute. But again, so is God, and the second refrain has a similar effect to the first, God as saviour re-entering the poem as flat affirmation.

> In power and truth, almighty and eternal,
> Which on the sin reflects strange desolation
> With glory scourging all the sprites infernal,
> And uncreated hell with unprivation;
>> Depriv'd of human graces, not divine,
>> Even there appears this saving God of mine.

What the presence of God can do is here described: he negates the negative, and he applies to Hell, the state of privation, its opposite—'unprivation'. And now the refrain can change, for the soul is thus not deprived of divine grace. But we still do not know *how* God has brought his grace to bear on the individual soul.

> For on this spiritual cross condemned lying,
> To pains infernal by eternal doom,
> I see my Saviour for the same sins dying,
> And from that hell I fear'd, to free me, come;
> Depriv'd of human graces, not divine,
> Thus hath his death rais'd up this soul of mine.

The rigour of his contemplation has now enabled the speaker to visualize Christ and has given him understanding of his grace. The contemplation is difficult: the first line of the stanza, heavy with consonants, gives a sense of difficulty barely overcome, but it is overcome—and in the fourth line the very punctuation, helping to define the movement, indicates firmness and confidence. In the refrain, the soul is still deprived of human grace, but it is triumphant partaker of divine grace, and the word 'Thus' at the start of the last line makes the appearance of God no longer the illogicality it was in the first stanza but something logical and inevitable. God saves by pains that are greater than those that were experienced by man in the first stanza, and the mirror becomes an instrument no longer of chastisement but of forgiveness and divine compassion. This is one of the great religious poems because the grave, strong, agonized mind is exercised to the full, working *with* the feeling throughout the meditation. The feeling is tense and clenched and never self-indulgent: faith provides it with hope, but it calls on the mind to explain how that hope can be fulfilled. And the needed assurance of God's saving power does not remain merely the illogical assertion of faith: it is embodied in the entire complex experience of the poem.

The last poem in *Caelica*, 'Sion lies waste,' bears certain resemblances to it; both are written in the same stanza-pattern, with the insistent refrain that finally changes and the sonority of the Latinate double rhymes, and both share the theme of man's degeneration. But here we do not have a description of Hell in an individual soul; instead the poem speaks about the corruption of social man.

> Sion lies waste, and thy Jerusalem,
> O Lord, is fall'n to utter desolation,
> Against thy prophets and thy holy men,
> The sin hath wrought a fatal combination,
> > Profan'd thy name, thy worship overthrown,
> > And made thee living Lord, a God unknown.

In this poem the simplicity of language, the directness of tone, and the lively variations in the verse movement, all serve to insist on the personal grief behind the public utterance. It is still a grief, however, that can sharply analyse: Greville never allows his feeling to eliminate his mind. God is a 'living Lord', a 'living light', but man's degeneration has its own life too, like the chemical changes in a rotting apple, and the multiplicity of that life must be itemized and described so that it may be recognized and rejected.

And rejected for what?

> That sensual unsatiable vast womb
> Of thy seen Church, thy unseen Church disgraceth.

The unseen Church is the abstraction, the ideal, the Form of what the seen Church should be. Again we see the Platonism which dominated Greville, and has dominated much of Christianity; and later we have God once more as exemplary mirror, his image being a 'sinless pure impression'. An abstraction cannot change, yet paradoxically God is an abstraction that is living, and he is not subject on the one hand to the state of inertia implied by the purely theoretical abstractions or on the other to the state of flux implied by the temporally living.

But in this poem God is a hope, rather than the present fact that he was in 'Down in the depth.' Greville ends imploring 'sweet Jesus, fill up time, and come,' but the tone does not have the assurance of the end of the earlier poem: there is still desperation behind the grief, desperation in the attitude that must reject all of life and find in it only corruption, interpreting absurdity as wickedness, seeing the only way to live as 'maids in earth's adulterous bed,' and holding out for an abstraction of complete purity which can never be possessed on earth.

The idea that life is vanity was held by most intelligent men of the Renaissance. Yet many of them evidently did not reinforce their thought with their feelings: life is vanity, perhaps, but meanwhile they could turn to an enjoyment of the world, for which they could always repent on the deathbed. Greville is different, I think, because his thought is reinforced by a propensity to despair. He was too strict, too honest with himself, too consistent, to disregard what both his mind and his emotions told him. In the last poems of *Caelica*, much of the greatness lies in the clarity and strength of the poignancy he gives to the despair that can be cured only by the end of life. And in these poems, too, the body cries out in pain at the rejections it is being forced to make, and in the note of the cry we recognize the very humanity it is a cry against.

Caelica

Caelica[1]

I

Love, the delight of all well-thinking minds;
Delight, the fruit of virtue dearly lov'd;
Virtue, the highest good, that reason finds;
Reason, the fire wherein men's thoughts be prov'd;
   Are from the world by Nature's power bereft,
   And in one creature, for her glory, left.

Beauty, her cover is, the eyes' true pleasure;
In honour's fame she lives, the ears' sweet music;
Excess of wonder grows from her true measure;
Her worth is passion's wound, and passion's physic;
   From her true heart, clear springs of wisdom flow,
   Which imag'd in her words and deeds, men know.

Time fain would stay, that she might never leave her,
Place doth rejoice, that she must needs contain her,
Death craves of Heaven, that she may not bereave her,
The Heavens know their own, and do maintain her;
   Delight, love, reason, virtue let it be,
   To set all women light, but only she.

[1] As Sidney's sonnet sequence was addressed to Stella (star), so Greville's early poems are addressed to Caelica (celestial one). However, *Caelica* is neither a sequence nor mainly sonnets. Moreover, some of the poems are addressed to girls called Myra and Cynthia, some to God, and others have no relevance to anyone celestial, sacred or profane. It is a convenient catch-all title.

II

Fair dog, which so my heart dost tear asunder,
That my life's blood, my bowels overfloweth,
Alas, what wicked rage conceal'st thou under
These sweet enticing joys, thy forehead showeth?

Me, whom the light-wing'd god of long hath chased,
Thou hast attain'd, thou gav'st that fatal wound,
Which my soul's peaceful innocence hath rased,[1]
And reason to her servant humour bound.

Kill therefore in the end, and end my anguish,
Give me my death, methinks even time upbraideth
A fulness of the woes, wherein I languish:
Or if thou wilt I live, then pity pleadeth
    Help out of thee, since Nature hath revealed,
    That with thy tongue thy bitings may be healed.

III

More than most fair, full of that heavenly fire,
Kindled above to show the Maker's glory,
Beauty's first born, in whom all powers conspire,
To write the Graces' life, and Muses' story.
    If in my heart all saints else be defaced,
    Honour the shrine, where you alone are placed.

Thou window of the sky, and pride of spirits,
True character of honour in perfection,
Thou heavenly creature, judge of earthly merits,
And glorious prison of man's pure affection,
    If in my heart all nymphs else be defaced,
    Honour the shrine, where you alone are placed.

[1] *rased:* erased

[46]

IV

You little stars that live in skies,
And glory in Apollo's glory,
In whose aspects conjoined lies
The Heavens' will, and Nature's story,
Joy to be liken'd to those eyes,
Which eyes make all eyes glad, or sorry,
    For when you force thoughts from above
    These overrule your force by love.

And thou O Love, which in these eyes
Hast married reason with affection,
And made them saints of beauty's skies,
Where joys are shadows of perfection,
Lend me thy wings that I may rise
Up not by worth but thy election;
    For I have vow'd in strangest fashion,
    To love, and never seek compassion.

V

Who trusts for trust, or hopes of love for love,
Or who belov'd in Cupid's laws doth glory;
Who joys in vows, or vows not to remove,
Who by this light god, hath not been made sorry;
    Let him see me eclipsed from my sun,
    With shadows of an earth quite overrun.

Who thinks that sorrows felt, desires[1] hidden,
Or humble faith with constant honour armed,
Can keep love from the fruit that is forbidden,
(Change I do mean by no faith to be charmed,)
    Looking on me, let him know, love's delights
    Are treasures hid in caves, but kept with sprites.[2]

[1] *desires* three syllables. Greville scans most -ire endings as two syllables, though not always. He is also inconsistent in the value he gives a word like 'power', which may be one or two syllables.   [2] *but kept with sprites:* but guarded by spirits

VI

Eyes, why did you bring unto me those graces,
Grac'd to yield wonder out of her true measure,
Measure of all joys, stay to fancy-traces,[1]
    Model of pleasure?

Reason is now grown a disease in reason,
Thoughts knit upon thoughts free alone to wonder,
Sense is a spy, made to do fancy treason,
    Love go I under.

Since then eyes' pleasure to my thoughts betray me,
And my thoughts reason's level have defaced;
So that all my powers to be hers, obey me,
    Love be thou graced.

Grac'd by me, love? No, by her that owes me.[2]
She that an angel's spirit hath retained
In Cupid's fair sky, which her beauty shows me,
    Thus have I gained.

VII

The world,[3] that all contains, is ever moving,
The stars within their spheres for ever turned,
Nature (the queen of change) to change is loving,
And form to matter new, is still adjourned.[4]

[1] *stay to fancy-traces:* 'her graces are the guides by which his fancy traces its courses' (G. Bullough, *Poems and Dramas of Fulke Greville*, Oliver and Boyd).

[2] *So that ... owes me:* so that I may command all my powers to be hers, love had better be blest. Blest by me? No, by her that owns me ...

[3] *the world:* Bullough points out that this means the universe.

[4] *adjourned:* transferred.

Fortune our fancy-god, to vary liketh,
Place is not bound to things within it placed,
The present time upon time passed striketh,
With Phoebus' wandering course the earth is graced.

The air still moves, and by its moving cleareth,
The fire up ascends, and planets feedeth,[1]
The water passeth on, and all lets weareth,[2]
The earth stands still, yet change of changes breedeth;

Her plants, which summer ripes, in winter fade,
Each creature in unconstant mother lieth,[3]
Man made of earth, and for whom earth is made,
Still dying lives, and living ever dieth;
    Only like fate sweet Myra never varies,
    Yet in her eyes the doom of all change carries.

VIII

Self-pity's tears, wherein my hope lies drown'd,
Sighs from thought's fire, where my desires languish,
Despair by humble love of beauty crown'd,
Furrows not worn by time, but wheels of anguish;
    Dry up, smile, joy, make smooth, and see
    Furrows, despairs, sighs, tears, in beauty be.

Beauty, out of whose clouds my heart tears rained,
Beauty, whose niggard fire sighs' smoke did nourish,
Beauty, in whose eclipse despairs remained,
Beauty, whose scorching beams make wrinkles flourish;
    Time hath made free of tears, sighs, and despair,
    Writing in furrows deep; *she once was fair*.[4]

[1] *The fire up ascends, and planets feedeth:* fires on earth rise up and nourish the
stars.   [2] *all lets weareth:* wears away all bounds.
   [3] *Each . . . lieth:* the unconstant mother is the earth, in which the plants are
rooted, and of which man is made, etc.
   [4] second stanza: She, beautiful, was unkind, and caused my tears, sighs, despairs,
and furrows; but, now that she is old, time has admitted *her* to the company of
tears, sighs, despairs, and furrows.

IX

O Love, thou mortal sphere of powers divine,
The paradise of nature in perfection,
What makes thee thus thy kingdom undermine,
Veiling thy glories under woe's reflection?
    Tyranny counsel out of fear doth borrow,
    To think her kingdom safe in fear and sorrow.

If I by nature, wonder and delight,
Had not sworn all my powers to worship thee,
Justly mine own revenge receive I might,
And see thee, tyrant, suffer tyranny:
    See thee thy self-despair, and sorrow breeding,
    Under the wounds of woe and sorrow bleeding.

For sorrow holds man's life to be her own,
His thoughts her stage, where tragedies she plays,
Her orb[1] she makes his reason overthrown,
His love foundations for her ruins[2] lays;
    So as while love will torments of her borrow,
    Love shall become the very love of sorrow.

Love therefore speak to Caelica for me,
Show her thy self in everything I do;
Safely thy powers she may in others see,
And in thy power see her glories too;
    Move her to pity, stay her from disdain,
    Let never man love worthiness in vain.

---

[1] *orb:* world.
[a] *foundations for her ruins* is the object of 'lays'.
[2] *ruins:* 'ruinous practices' (Bullough).

X

Love, of man's wandering thoughts the restless being,[1]
Thou from my mind with glory wast invited,
Glory of those fair eyes, where all eyes, seeing
Virtue's and beauty's riches, are delighted;
What angel's pride, or what self-disagreeing,
What dazzling brightness hath your beams benighted,
    That fallen thus from those joys which you aspired,
    Down to my darken'd mind you are retired?

Within which mind since you from thence ascended,
Truth clouds itself, wit serves but to resemble,[2]
Envy is king, at others' good offended,
Memory doth worlds of wretchedness assemble,
Passion to ruin passion is intended,
My reason is but power to dissemble;
    Then tell me Love, what glory you divine
    Yourself can find within this soul of mine?

Rather go back unto that heavenly choir[3]
Of Nature's riches, in her beauties placed,
And there in contemplation feed desire,
Which till it wonder, is not rightly graced;
For those sweet glories, which you do aspire,
Must as ideas[4] only be embraced,
    Since excellence in other form enjoyed,
    Is by descending to her saints destroyed.

[1] *being:* essence.

[2] *to resemble:* to note resemblances.

[3] *choir:* company; angelic order.

[4] *ideas:* here has full Platonic weight. Involvement with the particular is a descent.

XI

Juno, that on her head Love's livery carried,
Scorning to wear the marks of Io's pleasure,[1]
Knew while the boy in Equinoctial tarried,
His heats would rob the heaven of heavenly treasure,[2]
Beyond the Tropics she the boy doth banish,
Where smokes must warm, before his fire do blaze,[3]
And children's thoughts not instantly grow mannish,
Fear keeping lust there very long at gaze:
But see how that poor goddess was deceived,
For women's hearts far colder there[4] than ice,
When once the fire of lust they have received,
With two extremes so multiply the vice,
    As neither party satisfying other,
    Repentance still becomes desire's mother.

XII

Cupid, thou naughty boy, when thou wert loathed,
Naked and blind, for vagabonding noted,
Thy nakedness I in my reason clothed,
Mine eyes I gave thee, so was I devoted.

Fie, wanton, fie; who would show children kindness?
No sooner he into mine eyes was gotten,
But straight he clouds them with a seeing blindness,
Makes reason wish that reason were forgotten.

[1] *Juno . . . Io's pleasure:* Jupiter slept with Io, and turned her into a heifer to conceal her from the jealousy of Juno, but it was Juno who wore the horns of cuckoldry.

[2] *Knew . . . heavenly treasure:* the boy is Cupid, and the heats are those of love, which are stronger than those of the equatorial sun.

[3] *Where . . . do blaze:* warm smoke, preceding fire, is appropriate to youth.

[4] *there:* in the North.

From thence to Myra's eyes the wanton strayeth,
Where while I charge him with ungrateful measure,
So with fair wonders he mine eyes betrayeth,
That my wounds, and his wrongs, become my pleasure;
    Till for more spite to Myra's heart he flieth,
    Where living to the world, to me he dieth.

XIII

Cupid, his boy's play many times forbidden
By Venus, who thinks Mars' best manhood boyish,
While he shot all, still for not shooting chidden,[1]
Weeps himself blind to see that sex so coyish.

And in this blindness wandereth many places,
Till his foe Absence, hath him prisoner gotten,
Who breaks his arrows, bow and wings defaces,
Keeps him till he his boy's play hath forgotten.

Then lets him loose, no god of years but hours,
Cures and restores him all things, but his blindness,
Forbids him nothing but the constant powers,
Where Absence never can have power of kindness:
    Ladies, this blind boy that ran from his mother,
    Will ever play the wag with one or other.

XIV

Why how now reason, how are you amazed?[2]
Is worth in beauty, shrin'd up to be loathed?
Shall nature's riches by yourself be razed?
In what but these can you be finely clothed?

---

[1] *Cupid . . . shooting chidden:* 'Mars is not virile enough for Venus, and Cupid has done his best, and shot all his arrows' (Bullough).
[2] *amazed:* bewildered.

[53]

Though Myra's eyes, glasses of joy and smart,
Daintily shadow'd, show forth love and fear,[1]
Shall fear make reason from her right depart?
Shall lack of hope the love of worth forbear?[2]

Where is the homage then that nature oweth?
Love is a tribute to perfection due,
Reason in self-love's livery bondage showeth,
And hath no freedom, Myra, but in you;
    Then worth, love, reason, beauty be content,
    In Myra only to be permanent.

XV

When gentle beauty's over-wanton kindness,
Had given love the liberty of playing,
Change brought his eyesight by and by to blindness,
Still hatching in excess her own decaying;
Then cut I self-love's wings to lend him feathers,
Gave him mine eyes to see, in Myra's glory,
Honour and beauty reconcil'd togethers
Of love, the birth, the fatal tomb and story.
Ah wag, no sooner he that sphere[3] had gotten,
But out of Myra's eyes my eyes he woundeth;
And, but[4] his boy's play having all forgotten,
His heat in her chaste coldness so confoundeth,
    As he that burns must freeze, who trusts must fear,
    Ill-quarter'd coats,[5] which yet all lovers bear.

---

[1] *love and fear:* i.e. in me.

[2] *forbear:* tolerate; endure.

[3] *that sphere:* that region (and we must remember that a sphere is governed by an angel).

[4] *but:* then.

[5] *coats:* i.e. heraldic coats.

XVI

Fie foolish earth, think you the heaven wants glory,
Because your shadows do yourself benight?
All's dark unto the blind, let them be sorry,
The heavens in themselves are ever bright.

Fie fond desire, think you that love wants glory,
Because your shadows do yourself benight?
The hopes and fears of lust, may make men sorry,
But love still in herself finds her delight.

Then earth stand fast, the sky that you benight
Will turn again, and so restore your glory;
Desire be steady, hope is your delight,
An orb wherein no creature can be sorry;
    Love being plac'd above these middle regions,[1]
    Where every passion wars itself with legions.[2]

XVII

Cynthia, whose glories are at full for ever,
Whose beauties draw forth tears, and kindle fires,
Fires, which kindled once are quenched never,
So beyond hope your worth bears up desires.

Why cast you clouds on your sweet looking eyes?
Are you afraid they show me too much pleasure?
Strong Nature decks the grave wherein it[3] lies,
Excellence can never be expressed in measure.[4]

[1] *middle regions:* 'between heaven and hell' (Bullough).
[2] *legions:* 'of diabolical passions' (Bullough).
[3] *it:* Nature.
[4] *in measure:* in moderation.

Are you afraid, because my heart adores you,
The world will think I hold Endymion's place?
Hippolytus, sweet Cynthia, kneel'd before you,
Yet did you not come down to kiss his face.
    Angels enjoy the heavens' inward choirs:
    Stargazers only multiply desires.

XVIII

I offer wrong to my beloved saint,
I scorn, I change, I falsify my love,
Absence and time have made my homage faint,
With Cupid I do everywhere remove.

I sigh, I sorrow, I do play the fool,
Mine eyes like weather-cocks, on her attend:
Zeal thus on either side she puts to school,
That will needs have inconstancy to friend.

I grudge, she saith, that many should adore her,
Where love doth suffer, and think all things meet,
She saith, All self-ness must fall down before her:
I say, Where is the sauce should make that sweet?
    Change and contempt (you know) ill speakers[1] be:
    Caelica: and such[2] are all your thoughts of me.

XIX

Ah silly Cupid, do you make it coy
To keep your seat in Cala's furrow'd face?
Think in her beauty what you did enjoy,
And do not service done you so disgrace.

[1] *ill speakers:* poor persuaders (a 'fair speaker' meant an orator).
[2] *such:* ill speakers, because they are full of change and contempt.

She that refus'd not any shaft you shot,
Lent dews to youth, and sparks to old desire;
If such flat homage be so soon forgot,
Many good fellows will be out of hire.

Good archers ever have two bows at least,
With beauty faded shoot the elder sort;
For though all be not to shoot at the best,
Yet archers with their butting-bows[1] make sport:
  The glory that men in good kingdoms see,
  Is when both young, and old in traffic be.

XX

Why how now Cupid, do you covet change?
And from a stealer to a keeper's state,
With barking dogs do you the coverts range,
That carried bread to still them but of late?

What shall we do that with your bow are wounded?
Your bow which blindeth each thing it doth hit,
Since fear and lust in you are so confounded,
As your hot fire bears water still in it.

Play not the fool, for though your dogs be good,
Hardy, loud, earnest, and of little sleep,
Yet mad desires with cries are not withstood,
They must be better arm'd that mean to keep:
  And since unweapon'd care makes men forlorn,
  Let me first make your dog an unicorn.[2]

[1] *butting-bows:* 'unbarbed shafts' (Bullough).
[2] *Let . . . an unicorn:* 'he offers to arm Cupid's dog by giving it, as a weapon, a horn, i.e. by cuckolding the husband' (Bullough).

[57]

XXI

Satan, no woman, yet a wandering spirit,
When he saw ships sail two ways with one wind,
Of sailors' trade he hell did disinherit:
The Devil himself loves not a steadfast mind.

The satyr when he saw the shepherd blow
To warm his hands, and make his pottage cool,
Manhood forswears, and half a beast did know,
Nature with double breath is put to school.

Cupid doth head his shafts in women's faces,
Where smiles and tears dwell ever near together,
Where all the arts of change give passion graces;
While these clouds threaten, who fears not the weather?
   Sailors and satyrs, Cupid's knights, and I,
    Fear women that swear, Nay; and know they lie.

XXII

I with whose colours Myra dress'd her head,
I, that wore posies of her own hand-making,
I, that mine own name in the chimneys read
By Myra finely wrought ere I was waking:
   Must I look on, in hope time coming may
    With change bring back my turn again to play?

I, that on Sunday at the church-stile found,
A garland sweet, with true-love knots in flowers,
Which I to wear about mine arm was bound,
That each of us might know that all was ours:
   Must I now lead an idle life in wishes?
    And follow Cupid for his loaves, and fishes?

I, that did wear the ring her mother left,
I, for whose love she gloried to be blamed,
I, with whose eyes her eyes committed theft,
I, who did make her blush when I was named;
    Must I lose ring, flowers, blush, theft and go naked,
    Watching with sighs, till dead love be awaked?

I, that when drowsy Argus fell asleep,
Like jealousy o'erwatched with desire,
Was even warned modesty to keep,
While her breath, speaking, kindled Nature's fire:
    Must I look on a-cold, while others warm them?
    Do Vulcan's brothers in such fine nets arm them?[1]

Was it for this that I might Myra see
Washing the water with her beauties, white?
Yet would she never write her love to me;
Thinks wit of change while thoughts are in delight?
    Mad girls must safely love, as they may leave,
    No man can print a kiss, lines may deceive.

XXIII

Merlin, they say, an English prophet born,
When he was young and govern'd by his mother,
Took great delight to laugh such fools to scorn,
As thought, by nature we might know a brother.

His mother chid him oft, till on a day,
They stood, and saw a corse to burial carried,
The father tears his beard, doth weep and pray;
The mother was the woman he had married.

[1] *Do Vulcan's ... arm them:* i.e. he is Mars.

Merlin laughs out aloud instead of crying;
His mother chides him for that childish fashion;
Says, Men must mourn the dead, themselves are dying,
Good manners doth make answer unto passion.

The child (for children see what should be hidden)
Replies unto his mother by and by,
'Mother, if you did know, and were forbidden,
Yet you would laugh as heartily, as I.

'This man no part hath in the child he sorrows,
His father was the monk that sings before him:
See then how nature of adoption borrows,
Truth covets in me, that I should restore him.
    True fathers singing, supposed fathers crying,
    I think make women laugh, that lie a-dying.'

XXIV

Painting, the eloquence of dumb conceit,
When it would figure forth confused passion,
Having no tables for the world's receipt,[1]
With few parts of a few, doth many fashion.
Who then would figure worthiness disgraced,
Nature and wit imprisoned, or sterved,
Kindness a scorn, and courtesy defaced,
If he do well paint want, hath well deserved.
    But who, his art in worlds of woe, would prove,
    Let him within his heart but cipher love.

XXV

Cupid, my pretty boy, leave off thy crying,
Thou shalt have bells or apples; be not peevish;
Kiss me sweet lad; beshrew her for denying;
Such rude denials do make children thievish.

[1] *tables for the world's receipt:* 'formula ... of all that exists in nature' (Bullough).

Did reason say that boys must be restrained?
What was it, tell: hath cruel honour chidden?
Or would they have thee from sweet Myra weaned?
Are her fair breasts made dainty to be hidden?

Tell me (sweet boy,) doth Myra's beauty threaten?
Must you say grace when you would be a-playing?
Doth she cause thee make faults, to make thee beaten?
Is beauty's pride in innocents' betraying?
   Give me a bow, let me thy quiver borrow,
   And she shall play the child[1] with love, or sorrow.

XXVI

Was ever man so overmatch'd with boy?
When I am thinking how to keep him under,
He plays and dallies me with every toy;
With pretty stealths, he makes me laugh and wonder.

When with the child, the child-thoughts of mine own
Do long to play and toy as well as he,
The boy is sad, and melancholy grown,
And with one humour cannot long agree.

Straight do I scorn and bid the child away
The boy knows fury, and soon showeth me
Caelica's sweet eyes, where love and beauty play,
Fury turns into love of that I see.
   If these mad changes do make children gods,
   Women, and children are not far at odds.

[1] *play the child:* weep.

XXVII

Cupid, in Myra's fair bewitching eyes,
(Where beauty shows the miracles of pleasure)
When thou lay'st bound for honour's sacrifice,
Sworn to thy hate, equality and measure,[1]

With open hand thou offeredst me her heart,
Thy bow and arrows, if I would conspire,
To ruin honour, with whose frozen art
She tyranniz'd thy kingdom of desire.

I glad to dwell, and reign in such perfections,
Gave thee my reason, memory, and sense,
In them to work thy mystical[2] reflections,[3]
Against which nature can have no defence;
    And wilt thou now to nourish my despair
    Both head and feather all thy shafts with fear?

XXVIII

You faithless boy, persuade you me to reason?
With virtue do you answer my affection?
Virtue, which you with livery and seisin[4]
Have sold and changed out of your protection.

When you lay flattering in sweet Myra's eyes,
And played the wanton both with worth and pleasure,
In beauty's field you told me virtue dies,
Excess and infinite in love, was measure.

[1] *Sworn . . . and measure:* 'bound with oaths to thy enemies, proportion and moderation' (Bullough).

[2] *mystical:* 'spiritually symbolical; . . . of dark import' (O.E.D.).

[3] *reflections:* i.e. they are reflected in her eyes.

[4] *livery and seisin:* 'more correctly, livery *of* seisin, lit. the delivery of property into the hands of a purchaser' (Bullough).

I took your oath of dalliance and desire,
Myra did so inspire me with her graces,
But like a wag that sets the straw on fire,
You running to do harm in other places,
    Sware what is felt with hand, or seen with eye,
    As mortal, must feel sickness, age, and die.

XXIX

Faction, that ever dwells
In courts where wit excels,
    Hath set defiance:
Fortune and love have sworn,
That they were never born,
    Of one alliance.

Cupid, that doth aspire
To be god of desire,
    Swears he gives laws:
That where his arrows hit,
Some joy, some sorrow it,
    Fortune no cause.

Fortune swears weakest hearts,
The books of Cupid's arts,[1]
    Turn with her wheel:
Senses themselves shall prove,
Venture hath place in love,
    Ask them that feel.

This discord it begot
Atheists, that honour not
    Nature, thought good;
Fortune should ever dwell
In courts, where wits excel:
    Love keep the wood.

[1] *The books ... arts* is in apposition to 'hearts'.

Thus to the wood went I
With love to live and die;
   Fortune's forlorn:
Experience of my youth
Thus makes me think the truth
   In desert born.

My saint is dear to me,
Myra herself is she,
   She fair, and true:
Myra that knows to move,
Passions of love with love:
   Fortune Adieu.

XXX

Rome, while thy senate governors did choose,
Your soldiers flourish'd, citizens were free,
Thy state by change of consuls did not lose,
They honour'd were that serv'd or ruled thee:

But after thy proud legions gave thee laws,
That their bought voices empire did bestow,
Worthiness no more was of election cause,
Authority her owners did not know.

Sweet Myra, while good will your friends did choose,
Passions were dainty, sweet desires free,
By one friend[1] marriage did no honour lose,
They were esteem'd, that serv'd or ruled thee:

[1] *by one friend:* with only one friend (i.e. besides your husband).

But after flattering change did give thee laws,
That her false voices did thy faith bestow,
Worthiness no more was of affection cause,
Desire did many heads like monsters show;
    Thus Rome and Myra acting many parts,
    By often changes lost commanding arts.

XXXI

Goodfellows[1] whom men commonly do call,
Those that do live at war with truth, and shame,
If once to love of honesty they fall,
They both lose their goodfellows,[2] and their name;

For thieves, whose riches rest in others' wealth,
Whose rents are spoils, and others' thrift their gain,
When they grow bankrupts in the art of stealth,
Booties to their old fellows they remain.

Cupid, thou free of[3] these goodfellows art:
For while man cares not who, so he be one,
Thy wings, thy bow, thy arrows take his part,
He neither lives, nor loves, nor lies alone;
    But be he once to Hymen's close yoke sworn,
    Thou straight brav'st this goodfellow with the horn.

XXXII

Heavens! see how bringing-up corrupts or betters;
Cupid long prentice to his mother bound,
Hath taken oath, only to scape her fetters,
That he will still like to herself be found.

---

[1] *goodfellows:* '(i) a thief, or trickster, (ii) a sociable person' (Bullough).
[2] *goodfellows:* 'here, friends' (Bullough).
[3] *free of:* admitted to the privileges of (as of a chartered company, corporation, or city). Cupid is of their company.

E   [65]

Which is fair in his youth, in old age painted,
Kind out of lust, and humble for his pleasure,
Not long agreeing with things long acquainted,
Covetous, yet prodigal of fame and treasure.

Now as they wrong themselves, that for it thunders
Blame sky, or air, wherein these tempests blow:
So doth he that at women's changes wonders,
Since strange it should not be that all men know:
    Therefore if Myra change as others do,
    Free her; but blame the son, and mother too.

XXXIII[1]

Cupid, thy folly blears sweet Myra's eyes,
For like the blind, that upwards look for light,
You fix those fatal stars on Fortune's skies,
As though such planets gave not Fortune might.

Base boy, what heart will do him sacrifice,
That wraps repentance in his greatest pleasure?
And his true servants under Fortune ties,
As though his own coin were no current treasure?

Must Danae's lap be wet with golden showers?
Or through the seas must bulls Europa bear?
Must Leda only serve the higher powers?
Base changeling boy, and wouldst thou have me swear,
    The well-known secrets of Astolfo's cup,
    Not to disclose, but with white wax seal up?[2]

[1] Bullough points out that there is a play on the two senses of the word 'fortune': 'wealth' and 'chance'.

[2] *The well-known . . . seal up:* 'the reference seems to be to *Orlando Furioso*, where the hero's lost sanity is enclosed in a cup which Astolfo goes to the moon to regain . . . Greville means that since Cupid has betrayed him he cannot be expected to remain in a state of amorous insanity for ever.' (Bullough).

XXXIV

The gods to show they joy not in offences,
Nor plague of human nature do desire,
When they have made their rods and whipped our senses,
They throw the rods themselves into the fire.

Then Cupid, thou whom man hath made a god,
Be like thy fellow gods in weight and fashion,
And now my faults are punish'd, burn the rod
In fires blown with many-headed passion.

Thy rod is Worth, in Myra's beauty plac'd,
Which like a sun hath power to burn another,
And though itself can no affections taste,
To be in all men else affection's mother:
    Therefore if thou wilt prove thyself a god,
    In thy sweet fires, let me burn this fair rod.

XXXV[1]

Cupid, my little boy, come home again,
I do not blame thee for thy running hence,
Where thou found'st nothing but desire's pain,
Jealousy, with self-unworthiness, offence.[2]

Alas, I cannot Sir, I am made lame,
I light no sooner in sweet Myra's eyes,
(Whence I thought joy and pleasure took their name)
But my right wing of wanton passion dies.

[1] the first four lines are spoken by the poet, the remainder by Cupid.
[2] *Jealousy . . . offence:* I find this line difficult, and do not understand the syntactical relation between the three nouns.

[67]

And I poor child am here instead of play,
So whipp'd and scourg'd with modesty and truth,
As having lost all hope to scape away,
I yet take pleasure to 'tice hither youth:
    That my school-fellows plagu'd as well as I,
    May not make merry, when they hear me cry.

XXXVI

Kings that in youth like all things else, are fine,[1]
Have some who for their childish faults are beaten;
When more years unto greater vice incline,
Some,[2] whom the world doth for their errors threaten:

So Cupid, you, who boast of prince's blood,
For women's prince-like weaknesses are blamed,
And common error, yet not understood,
Makes you for their new-fangleness,[3] defamed.

Poor women swear, they ignorant of harms,
With gentle minds perchance take easy motions;
Sweet nature yielding to the pleasing charms
Of man's false lust disguised with devotion;
    But which are worse, kings ill, or easily led,
    Schools of this truth are yet not brought a-bed.[4]

XXXVII[5]

A thief, risen early up to seek his prey,
Spieth a pretty boy, whereas he lay,
    Crying fast by a well:
    He wills him why to tell,
And swears to make him well, if that he may.

[1] *fine:* delicate.   [2] *Some:* i.e. kings have some.
[3] *new-fangleness:* changeableness.   [4] *brought a-bed:* delivered.
[5] This poem appears to be a metrical experiment. Perhaps it is an unfinished state; the relevance of the fable to what follows is hard to make out, and the same girl is referred to as both Myra and Caelica.

[68]

The pretty boy smileth, and thanketh the man,
Told him, that he hath fallen his father's can,
   All of gold in the deep
   Which loss did make him weep;
Prayeth him counsel keep; help if he can.

The man not for conscience, but only for hope,
Puts off his clothes, goes down by the rope,
   Meaning to have the cup,
   If he can get it up;
He spills that steals a sup; haste loseth hope.

For while in the water the false fellow sought,
The pretty boy steals his cloak, well was he taught:
   Wet comes the fellow up,
   He cannot find the cup;
His cloak is taken up; falsehood is nought.

Little lad Cupid, by night and by day,
Wonted in beauty's face wanton to play,
   Fast bound and prison'd lies,
   In Myra's stealing eyes,
Woefully whence he cries, to run away.

I asked the boy, the boy telleth his case,
He saith, that virtue seeks beauty's disgrace,
   Virtue that grieves to find,
   With what an humble mind,
Men are to beauty kind, and her deface.

Virtue thinks all this is long of my bow,
Which hiding her beauties do counterfeits show,
   And beauty virtues arm,
   With such a modest charm,
As my shafts do no harm: she can say, No.

[69]

I that was wont to make wisdom a toy,
Virtue a pastime, am now made a boy,
    I am thrown from the heart,
    Banish'd is passion's art,
Neither may I depart, nor yet enjoy.

This was the cause, he said, made him complain,
He swears, if I help him, to help me again;
    And straightways offers me,
    If virtue conquer'd be,
Beauty and pleasure free; joy without pain.

I glad, not for pity, but hope of the prize,
And proud of this language from Caelica's eyes,
    Threw off my liberty,
    Hoping that blessed I,
Shall with sweet Cupid fly, in beauty's skies.

But when in my heart I had pieced[1] his bow,
And on the air of my thoughts made his wings go,
    The little lad fears the rod,
    He is not there a god,
I and delight are odd: Myra says, No.

The flint keepeth fire, the lad he says true,
But bellows it will not be kindled by you;
    He that takes stars with staves,
    Yet hath not all he craves;
Love is not his that raves: hope is untrue.[2]

XXXVIII

Caelica, I overnight was finely used,
Lodg'd in the midst of paradise, your heart:
Kind thoughts had charge I might not be refused,
Of every fruit and flower I had part.

---

[1] *pieced:* mended.   [2] The last stanza is spoken by Myra-Caelica.

But curious knowledge, blown with busy flame,
The sweetest fruits had down in shadows hidden,
And for it found mine eyes had seen the same,
I from my paradise was straight forbidden.

Where that cur, Rumour, runs in every place,
Barking with Care, begotten out of Fear;
And glassy Honour, tender of Disgrace,
Stands Seraphin to see I come not there;
    While that fine soil, which all these joys did yield,
    By broken fence is prov'd a common field.

XXXIX

The pride of flesh by reach of human wit,
Did purpose once to overreach the sky;
And where before God drown'd the world for it,
Yet Babylon it built up, not to die.

God knew these fools how foolishly they wrought,
That destiny with policy would break,
Straight none could tell his fellow what he thought,
Their tongues were chang'd, and men not taught to speak;

So I that heavenly peace would comprehend,
In mortal seat of Caelica's fair heart,
To babylon myself there, did intend,
With natural kindness, and with passion's art:
    But when I thought myself of herself free,[1]
    All's chang'd: she understands all men but me.

XL

The nurse-life wheat[2] within his green husk growing,
Flatters our hope and tickles our desire,
Nature's true riches in sweet beauties showing,
Which set all hearts, with labour's love, on fire.

[1] *free:* see note [3] page 65.   [2] *the nurse-life wheat:* the wheat that nourishes life.

No less fair is the wheat when golden ear
Shows unto hope the joys of near enjoying:
Fair and sweet is the bud, more sweet and fair
The rose, which proves that time is not destroying.

Caelica, your youth, the morning of delight,
Enamel'd o'er with beauties white and red,
All sense and thoughts did to belief invite,
That love and glory there are brought to bed;
    And your ripe year's love-noon (he[1] goes no higher)
    Turns all the spirits of man into desire.[2]

XLI

Alas poor soul, think you to master love,
With constant faith; do you hope true devotion
Can stay that god-head, which lives but to move,
And turn men's hearts, like vanes, with outward motion.

No; proud desire thou runn'st misfortune's way,
Love is to hers, like vessels made of glass;
Delightful while they do not fall away;
But broken, never brought to that it was.

When honour's audit calls for thy receipt,
And chargeth on thy head much time misspent;
Nature corrupted by thy vain conceit,
Thy reason servile, poor, and passion-rent,

What shall be thy excuse, what canst thou say?
That thou hast erred out of love and wonder?
No heretic, thou Cupid dost betray
And with religion wouldst bring princes under;

---

[1] *he:* i.e. the sun.

[2] *Turns . . . into desire:* 'The image is of the sun transforming the earth's moisture into vapour' (Bullough); and see LXIII, l. 13, p. 91.

By merit banish chance from beauty's sky,
Set other laws in women's hearts, than will;
Cut change's wings, that she no more may fly,
Hoping to make that constant, which is ill;
    Therefore the doom is, wherein thou must rest,
    Myra that scorns thee, shall love many best.

XLII

Pelius, that loth was Thetis to forsake,
Had counsel from the gods to hold her fast,
Forewarn'd what loathsome likeness she would take,
Yet, if he held, come to herself at last.
    He held; the snakes, the serpents and the fire,
    No monsters prov'd, but travails of desire.

When I beheld how Caelica's fair eyes,
Did show her heart to some, her wit to me;
Change, that doth prove the error is not wise,
In her mis-shape made me strange visions see,
    Desire held fast, till love's unconstant zone,
    Like Gorgon's head transform'd her heart to stone.

From stone she turns again into a cloud,
Where water still had more power than the fire,
And I poor Ixion to my Juno vow'd,
With thoughts to clip her, clipp'd my own desire:
    For she was vanish'd, I held nothing fast,
    But woes to come, and joys already past.

This cloud straight makes a stream, in whose smooth face,
While I the image of myself did glass,
Thought-shadows I, for beauty did embrace,
Till stream and all except the cold did pass;
    Yet faith held fast, like foils where stones be set,
    To make toys dear, and fools more fond to get.[1]

    [1] *fools more fond to get:* to beget fools even fonder.

Thus our desires besides each inward throe,
Must pass the outward toils of chance, and fear,
Against the streams of real truths they go,
With hope alone to balance all they bear,
    Spending the wealth of nature in such fashion,
    As good and ill luck, equally breeds passion.

Thus our delights, like fair shapes in a glass,
Though pleasing to our senses, cannot last,
The metal breaks, or else the visions pass,
Only our griefs in constant moulds are cast:
    I'll hold no more, false Caelica, live free;
    Seem fair to all the world, and foul to me.

XLIII

Caelica, when you look down into your heart,
And see what wrongs my faith endureth there,
Hearing the groans of true love, loath to part,
You think they witness of your changes bear.

And as the man that by ill neighbours dwells,
Whose curious eyes discern those works of shame,
Which busy rumour to the people tells,
Suffers for seeing those dark springs of fame.

So I because I cannot choose but know,
How constantly you have forgotten me,
Because my faith doth like the sea-marks show,
And tell the strangers where the dangers be,
    I, like the child, whom nurse hath overthrown,
    Not crying, yet am whipp'd, if you[1] be known.

        [1] *you:* i.e. the wrongs you have done.

XLIV

The Golden Age was when the world was young,
Nature so rich, as earth did need no sowing,
Malice not known, the serpents had not stung,
Wit was but sweet affection's overflowing.

Desire was free, and beauty's first-begotten;
Beauty then neither net,[1] nor made by art,
Words out of thoughts brought forth, and not forgotten,
The laws were inward that did rule the heart.

The Brazen Age is now when earth is worn,
Beauty grown sick, Nature corrupt and nought,
Pleasure untimely dead as soon as born,
Both words and kindness[2] strangers to our thought:

If now this changing world do change her head,
Caelica, what have her new lords for to boast?
The old lord knows desire is poorly fed,
And sorrows not a wavering province lost,
    Since in the gilt age Saturn rul'd alone,
    And in this painted, planets every one.

XLV

    Absence, the noble truce
    Of Cupid's war:
    Where though desires want use,
    They honour'd are.
    Thou art the just protection,
    Of prodigal affection,
    Have thou the praise;
    When bankrupt Cupid braveth,[3]
    Thy mines his credit saveth,
    With sweet delays.

[1] *net:* netted.   [2] *kindness:* natural feeling.   [3] *braveth:* dresses splendidly; boasts.

Of wounds which presence makes
With beauty's shot,
Absence the anguish slakes,
But healeth not:
Absence records the stories,
Wherein Desire glories,
Although she burn;
She cherisheth the spirits
Where Constancy inherits
And passions mourn.

Absence, like dainty clouds,
On glorious bright,
Nature weak senses shrouds,
From harming light.
Absence maintains the treasure
Of pleasure unto pleasure,
Sparing with praise;
Absence doth nurse the fire,
Which starves and feeds desire
With sweet delays.

Presence to every part
Of beauty ties,
Where wonder rules the heart
There pleasure dies:
Presence plagues mind and senses
With modesty's defences,
Absence is free:
Thoughts do in absence venter
On Cupid's shadowed centre,
They wink and see.

But thoughts be not so brave,
With absent joy;
For you with that you have
Yourself destroy:

The absence which you glory,
Is that which makes you sorry,
And burn in vain:
For thought is not the weapon,
Wherewith thought's ease men cheapen,[1]
Absence is pain.

XLVI

Patience, weak fortun'd, and weak minded wit,
Persuade you me to joy, when I am banish'd?
Why preach you times to come, and joys with it,[2]
Since time already come, my joys have vanish'd?

Give me sweet Cynthia, with my wonted bliss,
Disperse the clouds that coffer up my treasure,
Awake Endymion, with Diana's kiss,
And then sweet patience, counsel me to measure.

But while my love feels nothing but correction
While carelessness[3] o'ershadows my devotion,
While Myra's beams show rival-like reflection,[4]
The life of patience then must be commotion;
　　Since not to feel what wrong I bear in this,
　　A senseless state, and no true patience is.

XLVII

Atlas upon his shoulders bare the sky,
The load was heavy, but the load was fair:
His sense was ravish'd with the melody,
Made from the motion of the highest sphere.

[1] *Wherewith . . . men cheapen:* see Introduction p. 25.
[2] *it:* refers to 'times'.　　　[3] *carelessness:* lack of concern.
[4] *While Myra's . . . reflection:* Myra is rival-like to Cynthia-Diana in being equally unkind.

[77]

Not Atlas I, nor did I heaven bear,
Caelica, 'tis true, once on my shoulder sat,
Her eyes more rich by many carats were
Than stars or planets, which men wonder at:
    Atlas bare heaven, such burdens be of grace,
    Caelica in heaven, is the angel's place.[1]

XLVIII

Mankind, whose lives from hour to hour decay,
Lest sudden change himself should make him fear;
For if his black head instantly wax'd gray,
Do you not think man would himself forswear?

Caelica, who overnight spake, with her eyes
'My love complains, that it can love no more,'
Showing me shame, that languisheth and dies,
Tyrannis'd by love, it tyrannis'd before;
    If on the next day Cynthia change and leave,[2]
    Would you trust your eyes, since her eyes deceive?

XLIX

Princes, who have (they say) no mind, but thought,
Whose virtue is their pleasure, and their end,
That kindness,[3] which in their hearts never wrought,
They like in others, and will praise a friend.

[1] *Caelica . . . angel's place:* 'She is his heaven, and he her ministering Angel: an Angel's place is in heaven, ergo . . . The implication is obvious.' (Bullough).

[2] *If . . . and leave:* It does not look as if Caelica and Cynthia are here different persons, as Myra and Cynthia-Diana are in XLVI; rather it seems that they are two names for one girl as in XXXVII where she is referred to as both Myra and Caelica.

[3] *kindness:* natural affection.

Cupid, who, people say, is bold with blindness,
Free of [1] excess, and enemy to measure,
Yet glories in the reverence of kindness,
In silent-trembling eloquence hath pleasure.

Princes we comprehend, and can delight,
We praise them for the good they never had;
But Cupid's ways are far more infinite,
Kisses at times, and court'sies make him glad:
   Then Myra give me leave for Cupid's sake,
   To kiss thee oft, that I may court'sy make.

L

Scoggin his wife by chance mistook her bed;
Such chances oft befall poor women-kind,
Alas poor souls, for when they miss their head,
What marvel it is, though the rest be blind?

This bed it was a lord's bed where she light,
Who nobly pitying this poor woman's hap,
Gave alms both to relieve, and to delight,
And made the golden shower fall on her lap.

Then in a freedom asks her as they lay,
Whose were her lips and breasts: and she sware, his:
For hearts are open when thoughts fall to play.
At last he asks her, whose her backside is?
   She vow'd that it was Scoggin's only part,
   Who never yet came nearer to her heart.

Scoggin o'erheard; but taught by common use,
That he who sees all those which do him harm,
Or will in marriage boast such small abuse,
Shall never have his nightgown furred warm:
   And was content, since all was done in play,
   To know his luck, and bear his arms away.

[1] *free of:* see note [3] p. 65.

[79]

Yet when his wife should to the market go,
Her breast and belly he in canvas dress'd,
And on her backside fine silk did bestow,
Joying to see it braver than the rest.

His neighbours ask'd him, why? and Scoggin sware,
That part of all his wife was only his:
The lord should deck the rest, to whom they are,
For he knew not what lordly fashion is.
    If husbands now should only deck their own,
    Silk would make many by their backs be known.

LI

Caelica, because we now in absence live,[1]
Which liv'd so long in free-born love at one,
Straight curious rumour doth her censure[2] give,
That our aspects[3] are to another zone.[4]

Yet Caelica, you know I do not change,
My heart bears witness that there is no cause,
Authority may bid good-will be strange,
But true desire is subject to no laws:
    If I have spoken to the common sense,[5]
    It envy kills, and is a wise offence.

[1] *Caelica ... absence live:* i.e. they are apart from each other.
[2] *censure:* 'opinion' (Bullough).
[3] *aspects:* the way heavenly bodies appear to those on earth.
[4] *zone:* region of the sky.
[5] *common sense:* common view.

LII

Away with these self-loving lads,
Whom Cupid's arrow never glads:
Away poor souls, that sigh and weep,
In love of those that lie asleep:
    For Cupid is a meadow-god,
    And forceth none to kiss the rod.

Sweet Cupid's shafts like destiny
Do causeless good or ill decree;
Desert is born out of his bow,
Reward upon his wing doth go;
    What fools are they that have not known,
    That love likes no laws but his own.

My songs they be of Cynthia's praise,
I wear her rings on holy days,
In every tree I write her name,
And every day I read the same.
    Where honour Cupid's rival is
    There miracles are seen of his.

If Cynthia crave her ring of me,
I blot her name out of the tree,
If doubt do darken things held dear,
Then well fare nothing once a year
    For many run, but one must win,
    Fools only hedge the cuckoo in.

The worth that worthiness should move,
Is love, that is the bow of love,
And love as well the foster can,
As can the mighty nobleman.
    Sweet saint 'tis true, you worthy be,
    Yet without love nought worth to me.

F

LIII

But that familiar things are never wonder,
What greater beauty than the heaven's glories?
Where Phoebus shines, and when he is gone under,
Leaveth in fairest stars man's fatal stories;
    Yet Venus chose with Mars the netty bed,
    Before that heavenly life, which Vulcan led.

Who doth intreat the winter not to rain,
Or in a storm the wind to leave his blowing?
Ladies, show you how Juno did complain,
Or Jupiter unto Europa going.
    Fair nymphs, if I woo Cynthia not to leave me,
    You know 'tis I myself, not she deceives me.

Masters that ask their scholars leave to beat them,
Husbands that bid their wives tell all they know,
Men that give children sweetmeats not to eat them,
Ladies, you see what destiny they go:
    And who intreats, you know intreats in vain,
    That love be constant, or come back again.

LIV

Light[1] rage and grief, limbs of unperfect love,
By over-acting ever lose their ends;
For grief while it would good affection move,
With self-affliction doth deface her friends;
    Putting on poor weak pity's pale reflection,
    Whereas good-will is stirr'd with good complexion.[2]

[1] *light:* 'Rage and Grief are volatile, irresponsible' (Bullough).
[2] *complexion:* appearance.

Rage again fond of her inflam'd desire,
Desire which conquers best by close invasion,
Forgetting light and heat live in one fire,
So overblows[1] the temper[2] of occasion,
    That scorch'd with heat, by light discovered,
    Untimely born is, and untimely dead.

Poor fools, why strive you then since all hearts feel
That idle chance so governs in affection,
As Cupid cannot turn his fatal wheel,
Nor in his own orb banish her[3] election?
    Then teach desire hope; not rage, fear, grief,
    Powers as unapt to take, as give relief.

LV

Cynthia, because your horns look diverse ways,
Now darken'd to the East, now to the West,
Then at full glory once in thirty days,
Sense doth believe that change is Nature's rest.

Poor earth, that dare presume to judge the sky;
Cynthia is ever round, and never varies,
Shadows and distance do abuse the eye,
And in abused sense truth oft miscarries:
    Yet who this language to the people speaks,
    Opinion's empire sense's idol breaks.[4]

[1] *overblows:* blows too hard on.
[2] *temper:* 'the particular degree of hardness and elasticity or resiliency imparted to steel by tempering' (O.E.D.).
[3] *her:* i.e. chance's
[4] *Yet who . . . idol breaks:* i.e. Yet who speaks this language to the people breaks opinion's empire, which is sense's idol.

LVI

All my senses, like beacons' flame,
Gave alarum to desire
To take arms in Cynthia's name,
And set all my thoughts on fire:
Fury's wit persuaded me,
Happy love was hazard's heir,
Cupid did best shoot and see
In the night where smooth is fair;
Up I start believing well
10 To see if Cynthia were awake;
Wonders I saw, who can tell?
And thus unto myself I spake;
Sweet god Cupid where am I,[1]
That by pale Diana's light:
Such rich beauties do espy,
As harm our senses with delight?
Am I borne up to the skies?
See where Jove and Venus shine,
Showing in her heavenly eyes
20 That desire is divine:
Look where lies the Milken Way,
Way unto that dainty throne,
Where while all the gods would play,
Vulcan thinks to dwell alone.[2]

[1] His speech extends from this line to line 24.

[2] One manuscript adds the following lines between lines. 24 and 25:

Shadowing it with curious art,
Nets of sullen golden hair,
Mars am I, and may not part,
Till that I be taken there.
Therewithal I heard a sound,
Made of all the parts of love,
Which did sense delight and wound;
Planets with such music move.
Those joys drew desires near.
The heavens blush'd, the white show'd red,
Such red as in skies appear
When Sol parts from Thetis' bed.

Then unto myself I said
Surely I Apollo am,
Yonder is the glorious maid
Which men do Aurora name,
Who for pride she hath in me
Blushing forth desire and fear,
While she would have no man see,
Makes the world know I am there.
I resolve to play my son,
And misguide my chariot fire:
All the sky to overcome,
And enflame with my desire:

I gave reins to this conceit,
Hope went on the wheel of lust:
Fancy's scales are false of weight,
Thoughts take thought[1] that go of trust,
I stepp'd forth to touch the sky,
30   I a god by Cupid dreams,[2]
Cynthia who did naked lie,
Runs away like silver streams;
Leaving hollow banks behind,
Who can neither forward move,
Nor if rivers be unkind,
Turn away or leave to love.
There stand I, like Arctic Pole,
Where Sol passeth o'er the line,[3]
Mourning my benighted soul,
40   Which so loseth light divine.
There stand I like men that preach
From the execution place,
At their death content to teach
All the world with their disgrace:
He that lets his Cynthia lie,
Naked on a bed of play,
To say prayers ere she die,[4]
Teacheth time to run away:
Let no love-desiring heart,
50   In the stars go seek his fate,
Love is only Nature's art,[5]
Wonder hinders love and hate.
    None can well behold with eyes,
    But what underneath him lies.[6]

[1] *take thought:* are anxious.
[2] *I a god by Cupid dreams:* the subject of 'dreams' is 'a god', which is in apposition to 'I'.
[3] *line:* 'Equator' (Bullough).
[4] *die:* have sexual orgasm.
[5] *Love . . . art:* love is the art of Nature alone.
[6] *None . . . him lies:* see Introduction (p. 28).

[85]

LVII

Caelica, you blame me that I suffer not
Absence with joy, authority with ease:
Caelica, what powers can nature's[1] inside blot?
They must look pale without that feel disease.

You say that you do like fair Tagus' streams,
Swell over those that would your channels choke;
Yielding due tribute into Phoebus' beams,
Yet not made dry with loss of vapour's smoke.

Caelica, 'tis true, birds that do swim and fly,
The waters can endure to have and miss:
Their feet for seas, their wings are for the sky,
Nor error is it, that of Nature is.[2]
    I like the fish bequeath'd to Neptune's bed,
    No sooner taste of air, but I am dead.

LVIII

The tree in youth proud of his leaves, and springs,[3]
His body shadow'd in his glory lays;
For none do fly with art,[4] or others' wings,
But they in whom all, save desire, decays;
    Again in age, when no leaves on them grow,
    Then borrow they their green of mistletoe.

Where Caelica, when she was young and sweet,
Adorn'd her head with golden borrow'd hair,
To hide her own for cold; she thinks it meet
The head should mourn, that all the rest was fair;
    And now in age when outward things decay,
    In spite of age, she throws that hair away.

[1] *nature's:* i.e. a human being's   [2] *that of Nature is:* what is a part of Nature.
[3] *springs:* shoots.   [4] *art:* artifice.

Those golden hairs she then us'd but to tie
Poor captiv'd souls which she in triumph led,
Who not content the sun's fair light to eye,
Within his glory their sense dazzeled:
　　And now again, her own black hair puts on,
　　To mourn for thoughts by her worths overthrown.

LIX

Whoever sails near to Bermuda coast,
Goes hard aboard[1] the monarchy of fear,[2]
Where all desires (but life's desire) are lost,
For wealth and fame put off their glories there.

Yet this isle poison-like, by mischief known,
Weans not desire from her sweet nurse, the sea;
But unseen shows us where our hopes be sown,
With woeful signs declaring joyful way.
　　For who will seek the wealth of Western sun,
　　Oft by Bermuda's miseries must run.

Who seeks the god of love, in beauty's sky,
Must pass the empire of confused passion,
Where our desires to all but horrors die,
Before that joy and peace can take their fashion.

Yet this fair heaven that yields this soul-despair,
Weans not the heart from his sweet god, affection;
But rather shows us what sweet joys are there,
Where constancy is servant to perfection.
　　Who Caelica's chaste heart then seeks to move,
　　Must joy to suffer all the woes of love.

　　　　[1] *hard aboard:* close to the shore of.
　　　　[2] *the monarchy of fear:* the island ruled by fear.

LX

Caelica, you said, I do obscurely live,
Strange to my friends, with strangers in suspect,
(For darkness doth suspicion ever give,
Of hate to men or too much self-respect)
   Fame you do say, with many wings doth fly,
   Who leaves himself, you say, doth living die.

Caelica, 'tis true, I do in darkness go,
Honour I seek not, nor hunt after fame:
I am thought-bound, I do not long to know,
I feel within, what men without me blame:
   I scorn the world, the world scorns me, 'tis true;
   What can a heart do more to honour you?

Knowledge and fame in open hearts do live,
Honour is pure heart's homage unto these,
Affection all men unto beauty give,
And by that law enjoined are to please:
   The world in two I have divided fit;
   Myself to you, and all the rest to it.

LXI

Caelica, while you do swear you love me best,
And ever loved only me,
I feel that all powers are oppress'd
By love, and love by destiny.

   For as the child in swaddling-bands,
When it doth see the nurse come nigh,
With smiles and crows doth lift the hands,
Yet still must in the cradle lie:
   So in the boat of fate I row,
10   And looking to you, from you go.

When I see in thy once-beloved brows,
The heavy marks of constant love,
I call to mind my broken vows,
And child-like to the nurse would move;

But love is of the Phoenix-kind,
And burns itself, in self-made fire,
To breed still new birds in the mind,
From ashes of the old desire:
    And hath his wings from constancy,
20   As mountains call'd of *moving*[1] be.

Then Caelica lose not heart-eloquence,
Love understands not, come again:
Who changes in her own defence,
Needs not cry to the deaf in vain.

Love is no true-made looking glass,
Which perfect yields the shape we bring,
It ugly shows us all that was,
And flatters every future thing.
    When Phoebus' beams no more appear,
30   'Tis darker than the day was here.

Change I confess it is a hateful power,
To them that all at once must think,
Yet Nature made both sweet and sour,
She gave the eye a lid to wink:

And though the youth that are estrang'd
From mother's lap to other skies,
Do think that Nature there is chang'd
Because at home their knowledge lies;
    Yet shall they see who far have gone,
40   That pleasure speaks more tongues than one.

[1] *moving:* 'such epithets are earned by the rarity of the phenomena they ascribe
to their subject' (Bullough).

[89]

The leaves fall off, when sap goes to the root,
The warmth doth clothe the bough again;
But to the dead tree what doth boot,
The silly man's manuring pain?

Unkindness may piece up[1] again,
But kindness either chang'd or dead,
Self-pity may in fools complain;
Put thou thy horns on other's head:
    For constant faith is made a drudge,
50   But when requiting love is judge.

LXII

Who worships Cupid, doth adore a boy,
Boys earnest are at first in their delight,
But for a new, soon leave their dearest toy,
And out of mind, as soon as out of sight,
    Their joys be dallyings and their wealth is play,
    They cry to have, and cry to cast away.

Mars is an idol, and man's lust, his sky;[2]
Whereby his glories still are full of wounds,
Who worship him, their fame goes far and nigh,
But still of ruin and distress it sounds.
    Yet cannot all be won, and who doth live,
    Must room to neighbours and succession give.

Those Mercurists[3] that upon humours work,
And so make others' skill, and power their own,
Are like the climates,[4] which far Northward lurk,
And through long winters must reap what is sown;
    Or like the masons, whose art building well,
    Yet leaves the house for other men to dwell.

[1] *piece up:* make up.   [2] *his sky:* the sky he lives in.
[3] *Mercurists:* i.e. those born under the influence of Mercury: traders, orators, politicians, thieves.
[4] *climates:* Bullough finds an alternate manuscript reading of 'Chimates' or 'Chymates', and queries 'Can these be Eskimos?'

Mercury, Cupid, Mars, they be no gods,
But human idols, built up by desire,
Fruit of our boughs, whence heaven maketh rods,
And babies too for child-thoughts that aspire:
    Who sees their glories, on the earth must pry;
    Who seeks true glory must look to the sky.

LXIII

The greatest pride of human kind is wit,[1]
Which all art out, and into method draws;[2]
Yet Infinite[3] is far exceeding it,
And so is chance, of unknown things the cause,
    The feet of men against our feet do move,[4]
    No wit can comprehend the ways of love.

He that direct on parallels doth sail,
Goes Eastward out, and Eastward doth return;
The shadowed man, whom Phoebus' light doth fail,
Is black like him, his heat[5] doth over-burn;
    The wheels of high desire with force do move,
    Nothing can fall amiss to them that love.

Vapours of earth which to the sun aspire,
As Nature's tribute unto heat or light,
Are frozen in the midst of high desire,
And melted in sweet beams of self-delight,
    And who to fly with Cupid's wings will prove,
    Must not bewail these many airs of love.

[1] *wit:* intelligence, the reason.

[2] *Which . . . method draws:* 'which creates every Art, and turns knowledge in[to] systems (methods)' (Bullough).

[3] *Infinite:* the Infinite.

[4] *The feet . . . do move:* "Nor can we understand how men at the Antipodes can walk 'upside down'." (Bullough.)

[5] *him, his heat:* i.e. him whom Phoebus' heat.

Men that do use the compass of the sea,
And see the needle ever Northward look,
Some do the virtue in the loadstone lay,
Some say, the stone it from the North star took,
    And let him know that thinks with faith to move,
    They once had eyes, that are made blind by love.

LXIV

Caelica, when I did see you every day,
I saw so many worths so well united,
As in this union[1] while but one did play,
All others' eyes both wondered and delighted:

Whence I conceiv'd you of some heavenly mold,
Since love, and virtue, noble fame and pleasure,
Contain in one no earthly metal could,
Such enemies are flesh and blood to measure.

And since my fall, though I now only see
Your back, while all the world beholds your face,
This shadow still shows miracles to me,
And still I think your heart a heavenly place:
    For what before was fill'd by me alone,
    I now discern hath room for everyone.

LXV

Caelica, when I was from your presence bound,
At first good will both sorrow'd and repined,
Love, faith, and nature felt restraint a wound,
Honour itself, to kindness yet inclined;

[1] *this union:* i.e. this union of 'worths'.

[92]

Your vows one way, with your desires did go,
Self-pity then in you did pity me,
Yea sex did scorn to be imprison'd so,
But fire goes out for lack of vent, we see.

For when with time, desire hath made a truce,
I only was exempt, the world left free,
Yet what win you by bringing change in use,
But to make current infidelity?
    Caelica, you say, you love me, but you fear,
    Then hide me in your heart, and keep me there.

LXVI

Caelica, you (whose requests commandments be)
Advise me to delight my mind with books,
The glass where art doth to posterity,
Show nature naked unto him that looks,
    Enriching us, shortening the ways of wit,
    Which with experience else dear buyeth it.

Caelica, if I obey not, but dispute,
Think it is darkness, which seeks out a light,
And to presumption do not it impute,
10 If I forsake this way of infinite;[1]
    Books be of men, men but in clouds do see,
    Of whose embracements centaurs gotten be.

I have for books, above my head the skies,
Under me, earth; about me air and sea:
The truth for light, and reason for mine eyes,
Honour for guide, and nature for my way.
    With change of times, laws, humours, manners, right;
    Each in their diverse workings infinite.

    [1] *this way of infinite:* this infinite way.

[93]

Which powers from that we feel, conceive, or do,
20   Raise in our senses thorough joy, or smarts,
All forms, the good or ill can bring us to,
More lively far, than can dead books or arts;
     Which at the second hand deliver forth,
     Of few men's heads, strange rules for all men's worth.

False antidotes for vicious ignorance,
Whose causes are within, and so their cure,
Error corrupting nature, not mischance,
For how can that be wise which is not pure?
     So that man being but mere hypocrisy,
30   What can his arts but beams of folly be?

Let him then first set straight his inward sprite,
That his affections in the serving rooms,[1]
May follow reason, not confound her light,
And make her subject to inferior dooms;
     For till the inward molds be truly plac'd,
     All is made crooked that in them we cast.

But when the heart, eyes' light grow pure together,
And so vice in the way to be forgot,
Which threw man from creation, who knows whither?
40   Then this strange building which the flesh knows not,
     Revives a new-form'd image in man's mind,
     Where arts reveal'd, are miracles defin'd.[2]

What then need half-fast helps of erring wit,
Methods, or books of vain humanity?
Which dazzle truth, by representing it,
And so entail clouds to posterity.
     Since outward wisdom springs from truth within,
     Which all men feel, or hear, before they sin.

[1] *That his affections . . . rooms:* i.e. they are servants to the 'inward sprite'.
[2] *Where . . . miracles defin'd:* 'where the arts studied by the regenerate mind are those of Divine Revelation, and where natural laws are considered as miracles' (Bullough).

LXVII

Unconstant thoughts where light desires do move,
With every object which sense to them shows,
Still ebbing from themselves to seas of love,
Like ill-led kings that conquer but to lose,
With blood and pain these dearly purchase shame,
    Time blotting all things out, but evil name.

The double heart that loveth itself best,
Yet can make self-love bear the name of friend,
Whose kindness only in his wit doth rest,
And can be all but truth, to have his end,
    Must one desire in many figures cast;
    Dissemblings then are known when they are past.

The heart of man mis-seeking for the best,
Oft doubly or unconstantly[1] must blot,[2]
Between these two the misconceit[3] doth rest,
Whether it ever were that lasteth not,
    Unconstancy and doubleness depart,
    When man bends[4] his desires to mend his heart.

LXVIII

While that my heart an altar I did make,
To sacrifice desire and faith to love,
The little boy his temples did forsake,
And would for me no bow nor arrow move.
    Dews of disgrace my incense did depress:
    That heat went in, the heart burnt not the less.

---

[1] *Oft doubly or unconstantly:* i.e. 'doubly,' as in stanza 2, or 'unconstantly,' as in stanza 1.

[2] *blot:* 'revise its attitude' (Bullough).   [3] *misconceit:* doubt.

[4] *bends:* one manuscript has 'binds'.

And as the man that sees his house oppress'd
With fire; and part of his goods made a prey,
Yet doth pull down the roof to save the rest,
Till his loss give him light to run away:
    So when I saw the bell on other sheep,
    I hid myself, but dreams vex them that sleep.

My exile was not like the barren tree,
Which bears his fruitless head up to the sky,
But like the trees whose boughs o'erloaden be,
And with self-riches bowed down to die;
    When in the night with songs, not cries, I moan,
    Lest more should hear what I complain of one.

LXIX

When all this All doth pass from age to age,
And revolution[1] in a circle turn,
Then heavenly justice doth appear like rage,
The caves do roar, the very seas do burn,
    Glory grows dark, the sun becomes a night,
    And makes this great world feel a greater might.

When love doth change his seat from heart to heart,
And worth about the Wheel of Fortune goes,
Grace is diseas'd, desert seems overthwart,[2]
Vows are forlorn, and truth doth credit lose,
    Chance then gives law, desire must be wise,
    And look more ways than one, or lose her eyes.

My age of joy is past, of woe begun,
Absence my presence is, strangeness my grace,
With them that walk against me, is my sun:
The wheel is turn'd, I hold the lowest place,
    What can be good to me since my love is,
    To do me harm, content to do amiss?

[1] *revolution:* 'recurrent period of time; epoch' (O.E.D.).
[2] *overthwart:* i.e. the opposite to what it should be.

[96]

LXX

Cupid did pine, Venus that lov'd her son,
Or lack'd her sport, did look with heavy heart:
The gods are call'd, a council is begun,
Delphos is sought, and Aesculapius' art.

Apollo said, Love is a relative,[1]
Whose being only must on others be;
As bodies do their shadows keep alive,
So Eros must with Anteros[2] agree;
    They found him out a mate[3] with whom to play,
    Love straight enjoy'd, and pin'd no more away.

Caelica, this image figures forth my heart,
Where Venus mourns, and Cupid prospers not,
For this is my affection's overthwart,
That I remember what you have forgot;
    And while in you myself I seek to find,
    I see that you yourself have lost your mind.

When I would joy, as I was wont to do,
Your thoughts are chang'd, and not the same to me;
My love that lacks her playfellow in you,
Seeks up and down, but blinded cannot see.
    The Boy hath stol'n your thoughts some other way,
    Where wanton-like they do with many play.

LXXI

    Love, I did send you forth enamell'd fair
    With hope, and gave you seisin and livery[4]
    Of beauty's sky, which you did claim as heir,
    By objects' and desires' affinity.

---

[1] *a relative:* a relative thing.   [2] *Anteros:* Eros' brother, god of mutual love.
[3] *a mate:* presumably Anteros.   [4] *seisin and livery:* see note [4] p. 62.

And do you now return lean with despair?
Wounded with rivals' war, scorch'd with jealousy?
Hence changeling; Love doth no such colours wear:
Find sureties, or at honour's sessions die.

Sir, know me for your own, I only bear
Faith's ensign, which is shame, and misery;
My paradise, and Adam's diverse were:
His fall was knowledge, mine simplicity.

What shall I do, Sir? do me prentice bind,
To knowledge, honour, fame or honesty;
Let me no longer follow womenkind,
Where change doth use all shapes of tyranny;
    And I no more will stir this earthly dust,
    Wherein I lose my name, to take on lust.

LXXII

Caelica, you that excel in flesh and wit,
In whose sweet heart love doth both ebb and flow
Returning faith more than it took from it,
Whence doth the change, the world thus speaks on, grow?

If worthiness do joy to be admired,
My soul, you know, only bewonders you;
If beauty's glory be to be desired,
My heart is nothing else; what need you new?

If loving joy of worths[1] beloved be,
And joys not simple, but still mutual,
Whom can you more love, than you have lov'd me?
Unless in your heart there be more than all;
    Since love no doomsday hath, where bodies change,
    Why should new be delight, not being strange?

[1] *joy of worths:* seems to be in apposition to 'loving'.

LXXIII[1]

Myraphill, 'tis true, I lov'd, and you lov'd me,
My thoughts as narrow as my heart, then were;
Which made change seem impossible to be,
Thinking one place could not two bodies bear.
This was but earnest youth's simplicity,
To fathom[2] nature[3] within passion's wit,
Which thinks her earnestness eternity,
Till self-delight makes change look thorough it:
You banish'd were, I griev'd, but languish'd not,
For worth was free and of affection sure;
So that time must be vain, or you forgot,
Nature and love, no vacuum can endure;[4]
    I found desert, and to desert[5] am true;
    Still dealing by it, as I dealt by you.

LXXIV[6]

    In the window of a grange,
    Whence men's prospects cannot range
    Over groves, and flowers growing,
    Nature's wealth, and pleasure showing;
    But on graves where shepherds lie,
    That by love or sickness die;
    In that window saw I sit,
    Caelica adorning it,

[1] The poem is addressed to Myraphill (lover of Myra) and so must be spoken by Myra herself.

[2] *fathom:* embrace, clasp.

[3] *nature:* human nature.

[4] *So that . . . endure:* 'Worth was sure of affection. So now it seems, that the time of our love was empty (an illusion), or else that you forgot how Nature and Love abhor a vacuum.' (Bullough).

[5] *desert:* As Bullough points out, this word means both 'deserving' and 'desertion'.

[6] Caelica and Myra are again names for the same person in this poem.

Sadly clad for sorrow's glory,
10 Making joy glad to be sorry:
Showing sorrow in such fashion,
As truth seem'd in love with passion,
Such a sweet enamel giveth
Love restrain'd, that constant liveth.
Absence, that bred all this pain,
Presence heal'd not straight again;
Eyes from dark to sudden light,
See not straight, nor can delight.
Where the heart revives from death,
20 Groans do first send forth a breath:
So, first looks did looks beget,
One sigh did another fet,[1]
Hearts within their breast did quake,
While thoughts to each other spake.
Philocell entranced stood,
Rack'd, and joyed with his good,
His eyes on her eyes were fixed,
Where both true love and shame were mixed:
In her eyes he pity saw,
30 His love did to pity draw:[2]
But love found when it came there,
Pity was transform'd to fear:
Then he thought that in her face,
He saw love, and promis'd grace.
Love calls his love to appear,
But as soon as it came near,
Her love to her bosom fled,
Under honour's burdens dead.
Honour in love's stead took place,
40 To grace shame,[3] with love's disgrace;
But like drops thrown on the fire,
Shame's restraints inflam'd desire:
Desire looks, and in her eyes,
The image of itself espies,

---

[1] *fet:* fetch.   [2] *draw:* i.e. draw close.   [3] *shame:* modesty.

[100]

Whence he takes self-pity's motions
To be Cynthia's own devotions;[1]
And resolves fear is a liar,
Thinking she bids speak desire,
But true love that fears, and dare
50 Offend itself with pleasing care,
So divers ways his heart doth move,
That his tongue cannot speak of love.
Only in himself he says,
How fatal are blind Cupid's ways,
Where Endymion's poor hope is,
That while love sleeps, the heavens kiss.
But silent love is simple wooing,
Even Destiny would have us doing.
Boldness never yet was chidden,
60 Till by love it be forbidden,
Myra leaves him, and knows best,
What shall become of all the rest.[2]

LXXV[3]

In the time when herbs and flowers,
Springing out of melting powers,
Teach the earth that heat and rain
Do make Cupid live again:

[1] *To be . . . devotions:* Bullough says that Caelica-Myra is here praying to
Cynthia; but in view of the comparison made between the lover and Endymion, I
find it likely that the girl herself is Cynthia: desired, she is Caelica; chaste, she is
Cynthia; abrupt, earthly, and confused, she is Myra.

[2] *all the rest:* 'all her conflicting desires' (Bullough).

[3] George Williamson compares this poem to Sidney's 'In a grove most rich of
shade', to which it obviously bears a close relation. 'In Greville the seductive
element is almost lost in the extension and complication of the love casuistry.
Sidney's descriptive praise of the lady is greatly reduced, and the pastoral setting
finds no place in the love casuistry. While a more hopeless Petrarchan atmosphere
is developed, the poem ends with a real problem in love casuistry and thus justifies
the argumentative resolution. Sidney's Song was broken by an action which also
completed its argument.' (George Williamson, *Seventeenth Century Contexts*, p. 67).

Late when Sol, like great hearts, shows
Largest as he lowest goes,
Caelica with Philocell
In fellowship together fell:
Caelica her skin was fair,
10   Dainty auburn was her hair;
Her hair Nature dyed brown,
To become the mourning gown,
Of hope's death which to her eyes,
Offers thoughts for sacrifice.
Philocell was true and kind
Poor, but not of poorest mind,
Though mischance to harm affected[1]
Hides and holdeth worth suspected,
He good shepherd loveth well,
20   But Caelica scorn'd Philocell.
Through enamell'd meads they went,
Quiet she, he passion-rent.
Her worths to him hope did move;
Her worths made him fear to love.
His heart sighs and fain would show,
That which all the world did know:
His heart sigh'd the sighs of fear,
And durst not tell her love was there;
But as thoughts in troubled sleep,
30   Dreaming fear, and fearing weep,
When for help they fain would cry,
Cannot speak, and helpless lie:
So while his heart, full of pain,
Would itself in words complain,
Pain of all pains, lover's fear,
Makes his heart to silence swear.
Strife at length those dreams doth break,
His despair taught fear thus speak:
    'Caelica, what shall I say?
40   You, to whom all passions pray,

          [1] *affected:* inclined.
           [102]

Like poor flies that to the fire,
Where they burn themselves, aspire:
You, in whose worth men do joy,
That hope never to enjoy,
Where both grace, and beauty's framed,
That love being[1] might be blamed.
Can true worthiness be glad,
To make hearts that love it, sad?
What means Nature in her jewel,
50 To show mercy's image cruel?
Dear, if ever in my days,
My heart joy'd in others' praise:
If I of the world did borrow,
Other ground for joy or sorrow:
If I better wish to be
But the better to please thee;
I say, if this false be proved,
Let me not love, or not be loved.
But when reason did invite
60 All my sense to Fortune's light;
If my love did make my reason,
To itself for thyself treason;[2]
If when wisdom showed me
Time and thoughts both lost for thee;
If those losses I did glory,
For I could not more lose, sorry;
Caelica then do not scorn
Love, in humble humour borne.[3]
Let not Fortune have the power,
70 Cupid's godhead to devour.
For I hear the wise men tell,
Nature worketh oft as well,

---

[1] *love being:* 'love' is a noun; I think the phrase means 'love's essence'.

[2] *If my love . . . treason:* i.e. if my love did make my reason treasonous to itself for your sake.

[3] *borne:* this strikes me as a more likely reading than 'born' (the original manuscript has 'borne', which could have either sense).

[103]

In those men whom chance disgraceth,
As in those she higher placeth.
Caelica, 'tis near a god,
To make even fortunes odd;
And of far more estimation,
Is creator, than creation.
Then dear, though I worthless be,
80   Yet let them to you worthy be,
Whose meek thoughts are highly graced,
By your image in them placed.'
    Herewithal like one oppress'd,
With self-burdens he did rest,
Like amazed were his senses,
Both with pleasure and offences.
Caelica's cold answers show,
That which fools feel, wise men know:
How self-pities have reflection,
90   Back into their own infection:
And that passions only move
Strings tun'd to one note of love;
She thus answers him with reason,
Never to desire in season;
'Philocell, if you love me,
(For you would beloved be)
Your own will must be your hire,
And desire reward desire.
Cupid is in my heart sped,[1]
100   Where all desires else are dead.
Ashes o'er love's flames are cast,
All for one is there disgrac'd.
Make not then you own mischance,
Wake yourself from passion's trance,
And let reason guide affection,
From despair to new election.'
    Philocell that only felt
Destinies which Cupid dealt;

[1] *sped:* destroyed, killed.

[104]

No laws but love-laws obeying,
110 Thought that gods were won with praying.
And with heart fix'd on her eyes,
Where love he thinks lives or dies,
His words, his heart with them leading,
Thus unto her dead love pleading:
'Caelica, if ever you
Loved have, as others do;
Let my present thoughts be glassed,
In the thoughts which you have passed,
Let self-pity, which you know,
120 Frame true pity now in you;
Let your forepass'd woe, and glory,
Make you glad them, you make sorry.
Love revengeth like a god,
When he beats he burns the rod:
Who refuse alms to desire,
Die when drops would quench the fire.
But if you do feel again
What peace is in Cupid's pain,
Grant me, dear, your wished measure,
130 Pains but pains that be of pleasure;
Find not these things strange in me,
Which within your heart we see;
For true honour never blameth,
Those that love her servants nameth.
But if your heart be so free,
As you would it seem to be,
Nature hath in free hearts placed
Pity for the poor disgraced.'
His eyes great with child with tears
140 Spies in her eyes many fears,
Sees he thinks, that sweetness vanish
Which all fears was wont to banish.
Sees, sweet Love, there wont to play,
Arm'd and dress'd to run away,
[105]

To her heart where she alone,
Scorneth all the world but one.
Caelica with clouded face,
Giving unto anger grace,
While she threat'ned him displeasure,
150 Making anger look like pleasure,
Thus in fury to him spake,
Words which make even hearts to quake:
'Philocell, far from me get you,
Men are false, we cannot let[1] you;
Humble, and yet full of pride,
Earnest, not to be denied;
Now us, for not loving, blaming,
Now us, for too much, defaming:
Though I let you posies bear,
160 Wherein my name cyph'red were,
For I bid you in the tree,
Cypher down your name by me:
For the bracelet pearl-like white,
Which you stole from me by night,
I content was you should carry
Lest that you should longer tarry,
Think you that you might encroach,
To set kindness more abroach?[2]
Think you me in friendship tied,
170 So that nothing be denied?
Do you think that I must live,
Bound to that which you will give?
Philocell, I say, depart,
Blot my love out of thy heart,
Cut my name out of the tree,
Bear not memory of me.
My delight is all my care,
All laws else despised are,

[1] *let:* 'ambiguous; (i) prevent you (from being false); (ii) suffer you. Probably the first meaning was intended.' (Bullough).

[2] *set . . . abroach:* pierce and leave running (i.e. like a beer keg).

I will never rumour move,
180   At least for one I do not love.'

Shepherdesses, if it prove,
Philocell she once did love,
Can kind doubt of true affection
Merit such a sharp correction?
When men see you fall away,
Must they wink to see no day?
It is worse in him that speaketh,
Than in her that friendship breaketh?
Shepherdesses, when you change,
190   Is your fickleness so strange?
Are you thus impatient still?
Is your honour slave to will?
They to whom you guilty be,
Must not they your error see?
May true martyrs at the fire
Not so much as life desire?
Shepherdesses, yet mark well,
The martyrdom of Philocell:
Rumour made his faith a scorn,
200   Him, example of forlorn[1],
Feeling he had of his woe,
Yet did love his overthrow;[2]
For that she knew love would bear,
She to wrong him did not fear;
Jealousy of rivals' grace,
In his passion got a place;
But Love, lord of all his powers,
Doth so rule this heart of ours,
As for our belov'd abuses,
210   It doth ever find excuses.
Love tears reason's law in sunder,
Love, is god, let reason wonder.

[1] *Him . . . forlorn:* i.e. Rumour made him an example of forlornless.
[2] *Feeling . . . overthrow:* i.e. though he felt his woe, he loved his overthrow.

[107]

For nor scorn of his affection,
Nor despair in his election,
Nor his faith damn'd for obeying,
Nor her change, his hopes betraying,
Can make Philocell remove,
But he Caelica will love.
    Here my silly song is ended,
220 Fair nymphs be you not offended,
For as men that travell'd far,
For seen truths, oft scorned are,
By their neighbours, idle lives,
Who scarce know to please their wives;
So though I have sung you more,
Than your hearts have felt before,
Yet that faith in men doth dwell,
Who travels constancy[1] can tell.

LXXVI[2]

Fortune, art thou not forc'd sometimes to scorn?
That see'st ambition strive to change our state?
As though thy sceptre slave to lust were born?
Or wishes could procure themselves a fate?

I, when I have shot one shaft at my mother,
That her desires afoot think all her own,
Then straight draw up my bow to strike another,
For gods are best by discontentment known.

And when I see the poor forsaken sprite,
Like sick men, whom the doctor saith must die,
Sometime with rage and strength of passion fight,
Then languishing enquire what life might buy:
    I smile to see desire is never wise,
    But wars with change, which is her paradise.

---

[1] *constancy:* 'the realm of constancy' (Bullough). But U. M. Ellis Fermor, in her modernization of *Caelica*, prints the line 'Who travels' constancy can tell.'
[2] spoken by Cupid.

LXXVII

The heathen gods finite in power, wit, birth,
Yet worshipped for their good deeds to men,
At first kept stations between heaven, and earth,
Alike just to the castle, and the den;
    Creation, merit, nature duly weighed,
    And yet, in show, no rule, but will[1] obeyed.

Till time, and selfness,[2] which turn worth to arts,
Love into compliments, and things to thought,
Found out new circles to enthrall men's hearts
By laws; wherein while thrones seem overwrought,[3]
    Power finely hath surpris'd this faith[4] of man,
    And tax'd his freedom at more than he can.[5]

For to the sceptres judges laws reserve
As well the practic, as expounding sense,
From which no innocence can painless swerve,
They being engines of omnipotence:
    With equal shows, then is not humble man
    Here finely tax'd at much more than he can?

Our modern tyrants, by more gross ascent,
Although they found distinction in the state
Of church, law, custom, people's government,
Mediums (at least) to give excess a rate[6]
    Yet fatally have tried to change this frame
    And make will law, man's wholesome laws but name.[7]

---

[1] *will:* their own wills (in the sense of selfwilledness, caprices, whims).

[2] *selfness:* self-centredness; selfishness.

[3] *seem overwrought:* i.e. they seem more restrained by laws than they really are.

[4] *this faith:* i.e. that kings are restrained by laws.

[5] *can:* 'can afford (without losing his freedom)' (Bullough).

[6] *rate:* limit.

[7] *man's . . . name:* i.e. man's wholesome laws surviving as mere words.

But when power once hath trod this path of might,
And found how place advantageously extended
Wanes, or confoundeth all inferiors' right
With thin lines hardly seen, but never ended;
    It straight drowns in this gulf of vast affections,
    Faith, truth, worth, law, all popular protections.

LXXVIII

The little hearts, where light-wing'd passion reigns,
Move easily upward, as all frailties do;
Like straws to jet, these follow princes' veins,
And so, by pleasing, do corrupt them too.
    Whence as their raising proves kings can create,
    So states prove sick, where toys bear staple-rate.[1]

Like atomi[2] they neither rest, nor stand,
Nor can erect; because they nothing be
But baby-thoughts, fed with time-present's hand,
Slaves, and yet darlings of authority;
    Echoes of wrong; shadows of princes' might;
    Which glow-worm-like, by shining, show 'tis night.

Curious of fame, as foul is to be fair;
Caring to seem that which they would not be;
Wherein chance helps, since praise is power's heir,
Honour the creature of authority:
    So as borne high, in giddy orbs of grace,
    These pictures are, which are indeed but place.[3]

---

[1] *where toys bear staple-rate:* where toys are valued at the same price as staple
goods.
[2] *atomi:* atoms.   [3] *but place:* rank alone.

And as the bird in hand, with freedom lost,
Serves for a stale,[1] his fellows to betray:
So do these darlings rais'd at princes' cost
Tempt man to throw his liberty away;
    And sacrifice law, church, all real things
    To soar, not in his own, but eagle's wings.

Whereby, like Aesop's dog, men lose their meat,
To bite at glorious shadows, which they see;
And let fall those strengths which make all states great
By free truths chang'd to servile flattery.
    Whence, while men gaze upon this blazing star,
    Made slaves, not subjects, they to tyrants are.

LXXIX

As when men see a blazing star appear,
Each stirs up others' levity to wonder,
In restless thoughts holding those visions dear,
Which threaten to rent government in sunder;
    Yet be but horrors, from vain hearts sent forth,
    To prophesy against anointed worth:

So likewise mankind, when true government
Her great examples to the world brings forth,
Straight in the error's native discontent,
Sees apparitions opposite to worth;
    Which gathers such sense out of envy's beams,
    As still casts imputation on supremes.

[1] *stale:* decoy.

LXXX[1]

Clear spirits, which in images set forth
The ways of Nature by fine imitation,
Are oft forc'd to hyperboles of worth,
As oft again to monstrous declination;[2]
    So that their heads must lin'd[3] be, like the sky,
    For all opinion's arts to traffic by.[4]

Dull spirits again, which love all constant grounds,
As comely veils for their unactiveness,
Are oft forc'd to contract, or stretch their bounds,
As active power spreads her beams more, or less:
    For though in Nature's wane these guests[5] come forth;
    Can place,[6] or stamp make current aught but worth?

---

[1] Hugh N. Maclean's summary of this difficult poem is useful. It 'seems to say that while poets like Sidney truly imitate nature in the images they make, are in fact capable of "fine imitation," less gifted poets (Greville may even mean "most men") are simply not engaged in an activity of the same kind, because their "dull" and "unactive" natures characteristically "love all constant grounds". That is, they are "captived to the trueth of a foolish world".' (The last phrase is a quotation from Sidney's *Defence of Poesy*.) (Hugh N. Maclean, 'Greville's "Poetic",' *Studies in Philology*, April 1964, LXI, pp. 179–180.)

[2] *Are oft . . . declination:* i.e. they are forced to distort in order to convey the essence of the real.

[3] *lin'd:* 'the image refers to the astronomical maps on which were marked for the benefit of sailors, etc., the positions and courses of planets and stars (e.g. ecliptic and equinoctial lines). The meaning is that the motions of an artist's imagination must be clearly charted or fixed in words.' (Bullough).

[4] *For all . . . by:* 'So that all kinds of human intelligence and opinion may deal with them' (Bullough).

[5] *these guests:* 'these temporary inmates of power' (Bullough).

[6] *place:* rank. The rest of the line uses a coining image.

LXXXI[1]

Under a throne[2] I saw a virgin sit,
The red, and white rose quarter'd in her face;[3]
Star of the North, and for true guards[4] to it,
Princes, Church, states, all pointing out her grace.
The homage done her was not born of wit,
Wisdom admir'd, zeal took ambition's place,
State in her eyes taught order how to fit,
And fix confusion's unobserving race.
   Fortune can here claim nothing truly great,
   But that this princely creature is her seat.

LXXXII

You that seek what life is in death,
Now find it air that once was breath.
New names unknown, old names gone:
Till time end bodies, but souls none.
   Reader! then make time while you be,
   But steps to your eternity.

LXXXIII[5]

Who grace, for zenith had, from whom no shadows grow,
Who hath seen joy of all his hopes, and end of all his woe,
Whose love belov'd hath been the crown of his desire,
Who hath seen sorrow's glories burnt, in sweet affection's
   fire:

[1] The poem is about Queen Elizabeth.
[2] *Under a throne:* i.e. under a throne's canopy.
[3] *The red . . . her face:* refers to the roses of Lancaster and York.
[4] *guards:* 'the two stars of the constellation of the Lesser Bear known astro-nomically as Beta and Gamma; also *guards of the pole*' (O.E.D.).
[5] Possibly an appeal to Queen Elizabeth, to restore him to favour.

If from this heavenly state, which souls with souls unites,
He be fall'n down into the dark despaired war of sprites;
Let him lament with me, for none doth glory know,
That hath not been above himself, and thence fall'n down
    to woe:
But if there be one hope left in his languish'd heart,
10 In fear of worse, if wish of ease, if horror may depart,
He plays with his complaints, he is no mate for me,
Whose love is lost, whose hopes are fled, whose fears for
    ever be.
Yet not those happy fears which show desire her death
Teaching with use a peace in woe, and in despair a faith:
No, no, my fears kill not, but make uncured wounds,
Where joy and peace do issue out, and only pain abounds.
Unpossible are help, reward and hope to me,
Yet while unpossible they are, they easy seem to be.
Most easy seems remorse, despair and death to me,
20 Yet while they passing easy seem, unpossible they be.
So neither can I leave my hopes that do deceive
Nor can I trust mine own despair, and nothing else receive.
Thus be unhappy men, blest to be more accurst;
Near to the glories of the sun, clouds with most horror
    burst.
Like ghosts rais'd out of graves, who live not, though they
    go,
Whose walking fear to others is, and to themselves a woe:
So is my life by her whose love to me is dead,
On whose worth my despair yet walks, and my desire is
    fed;
I swallow down the bait, which carries down my death;
30 I cannot put love from my heart, while life draws in my
    breath;
My winter is within which withereth my joy;
My knowledge, seat of civil war, where friends and foes
    destroy,
And my desires are wheels, whereon my heart is borne,
With endless turning of themselves, still living to be torn.

[114]

My thoughts are eagles' food, ordain'd to be a prey
To worth; and being still consum'd, yet never to decay.
My memory, where once my heart laid up the store
Of help, of joy, of spirits' wealth to multiply them more;
Is now become the tomb wherein all these lie slain,
40   My help, my joy, my spirits' wealth all sacrific'd to pain.
In Paradise I once did live; and taste the tree,
Which shadow'd was from all the world, in joy to shadow
      me.
The tree hath lost his fruit, or I have lost my seat,
My soul both black with shadow is, and over-burnt with
      heat:
Truth here for triumph serves, to show her power is great,
Whom no desert can overcome, nor no distress intreat.
Time past lays up my joy; and time to come my grief,
She ever must be my desire, and never my relief.
Wrong, her lieutenant is; my wounded thoughts are they,
50   Who have no power to keep the field, nor will to run
      away.
O rueful constancy, and where is change so base,
As it may be compar'd with thee in scorn, and in disgrace?
Like as the kings forlorn, depos'd from their estate,
Yet cannot choose but love the crown, although new kings
      they hate;
If they do plead their right, nay, if they only live,
Offences to the crown alike their good and ill shall give;
So (I would I were not) because I may complain,
And cannot choose but love my wrongs, and joy to wish in
      vain;
This faith condemneth me, my right doth rumour move,
60   I may not know the cause I fell, nor yet without cause love.
Then love where is reward, at least where is the fame
Of them that being, bear thy cross, and being not, thy
      name?
The world's example I, a fable everywhere,
A well from whence the springs are dried, a tree that doth
      not bear:

[115]

I like the bird in cage at first with cunning caught,
And in my bondage for delight with greater cunning taught.
Now owner's humour dies, I neither lov'd nor fed,
Nor freed am, till in the cage forgotten I be dead.
The ship of Greece, the streams and she be not the same[1]

70   They were, although ship, streams and she still bear their
        antique name.
The wood which was, is worn, those waves are run away,
Yet still a ship, and still a stream, still running to a sea.
She lov'd, and still she loves, but doth not still love me,
To all except myself yet is, as she was wont to be.
O, my once happy thoughts, the heaven where grace did
        dwell,
My saint hath turn'd away her face, and made that heaven
        my hell.
A hell, for so is that from whence no souls return,
Where, while our spirits are sacrificed, they waste not
        though they burn.
Since then this is my state, and nothing worse than this,

80   Behold the map of death-like life exil'd from lovely bliss,
Alone among the world, strange with my friends to be,
Showing my fall to them that scorn, see not or will not
        see.
My heart a wilderness, my studies only fear,
And as in shadows of curs'd death, a prospect of despair.
My exercise, must be my horrors to repeat,
My peace, joy, end, and sacrifice her dead love to intreat.
My food, the time that was; the time to come, my fast;
For drink, the barren thirst I feel of glories that are past;
Sighs and salt tears my bath; reason, my looking-glass,

90   To show me he most wretched is, that once most happy
        was.

[1] *The Ship ... the same:* Bullough quotes J. Hannah, *Courtly Poets*, 1870: 'The ship of Greece is clearly the famous ship in which Theseus returned after slaying the Minotaur. The Athenians professed to preserve it till the days of Demetrius Phalereus, the rotten timbers being carefully removed and renewed from time to time, so that it became a favourite question whether a ship of which every plank had been often changed could still be called the same ...'

Forlorn desires my clock to tell me every day
That time hath stolen love, life and all but my distress
    away.
For music heavy sighs, my walk an inward woe,
Which like a shadow ever shall before my body go:
And I myself am he, that doth with none compare,
Except in woes and lack of worth; whose states more
    wretched are.
Let no man ask my name, nor what else I should be;
For Grieve-Ill, pain, forlorn estate do best decypher me.

LXXXIV

Farewell sweet boy, complain not of my truth;
Thy mother lov'd thee not with more devotion;
For to thy boy's play I gave all my youth,
Young master, I did hope for your promotion.

While some sought honours, princes' thoughts observing,
Many woo'd Fame, the child of pain and anguish,
Others judg'd inward good a chief deserving,
I in thy wanton visions joy'd to languish.

I bow'd not to thy image for succession,[1]
Nor bound thy bow to shoot reformed kindness,[2]
Thy plays of hope and fear were my confession,[3]
The spectacles to my life was thy blindness;[4]
    But Cupid now farewell, I will go play me,
      With thoughts that please me less and less betray me.

[1] *succession:* progeny.

[2] *Nor bound . . . kindness:* 'Nor use Love's other arrows (of hate) for persecution;
an allusion to the persecution of the reformers under Mary, etc.' (Bullough).

[3] *confession:* creed.

[4] *The spectacles . . . to blindness:* i.e. the only way I could see anything was with
eyes blinded by love.

LXXXV

Love is the peace, whereto all thoughts do strive,
Done and begun with all our powers in one:
The first and last in us that is alive,
End of the good, and therewith pleas'd alone.

Perfection's spirit, goddess of the mind,
Passed through hope, desire, grief and fear,
A simple goodness in the flesh refin'd,
Which of the joys to come doth witness bear.

Constant, because it sees no cause to vary,
A quintessence of passions overthrown,
Rais'd above all that change of objects carry,[1]
A nature by no other nature known:
    For glory's of eternity a frame,[2]
    That by all bodies else obscures her name.

LXXXVI

The earth with thunder torn, with fire blasted,
With waters drown'd, with windy palsy shaken
Cannot for this with heaven be distasted,[3]
Since thunder, rain and winds from earth are taken:
Man torn with love, with inward furies blasted,
Drown'd with despair, with fleshly lustings shaken,
Cannot for this with heaven be distasted,
Love, fury, lustings out of man are taken.

Then man, endure thyself, those clouds will vanish;
Life is a top which whipping Sorrow driveth;
Wisdom must bear what our flesh cannot banish,
The humble lead, the stubborn bootless striveth:
    Or man, forsake thyself, to heaven turn thee,
    Her flames enlighten nature, never burn thee.

[1] *carry:* involve.   [2] *frame:* 'form, attribute, or emanation' (Bullough).
[3] *distasted:* offended, disgusted.

[118]

LXXXVII

When as man's life, the light of human lust,
In socket of his earthly lantern burns,
That all this glory unto ashes must,
And generation to corruption turns;
    Then fond desires that only fear their end,
    Do vainly wish for life, but to amend.

But when this life is from the body fled,
To see itself in that eternal glass,
Where time doth end, and thoughts accuse the dead,
Where all to come, is one with all that was;
    Then living men ask how he left his breath,
    That while he lived never thought of death.

LXXXVIII

Man, dream no more of curious mysteries,
As what was here before the world was made,
The first man's life, the state of Paradise,
Where Heaven is, or Hell's eternal shade,
    For God's works are like him, all infinite;
    And curious search, but crafty sin's delight.

The flood that did, and dreadful fire that shall,
Drown, and burn up the malice of the earth,
The divers tongues, and Babylon's downfall,
Are nothing to the man's renewed birth;
    First, let the Law plough up thy wicked heart,
    That Christ may come, and all these types depart.

When thou hast swept the house that all is clear,
When thou the dust hast shaken from thy feet,
When God's all-might doth in thy flesh appear,
Then seas with streams above thy sky do meet;
    For goodness only doth God comprehend,
    Knows what was first, and what shall be the end.

LXXXIX[1]

The Manicheans did no idols make,
Without themselves, nor worship gods of wood,
Yet idols did in their ideas take,
And figur'd Christ as on the cross he stood.
    Thus did they when they earnestly did pray,
    Till clearer faith this idol took away:

We seem more inwardly to know the Son,
And see our own salvation in his blood;
When this is said, we think the world is done,
And with the Father hold our portion good:
    As if true life within these words were laid,
    For him that in life, never words obey'd.

If this be safe, it is a pleasant way,
The cross of Christ is very easily borne:
But six days labour makes the sabbath day,
The flesh is dead before grace can be born.
    The heart must first bear witness with the book,
    The earth must burn, ere we for Christ can look.

XC

The Turkish government allows no law,
Men's lives and states depend on his behest;
We think subjection there a servile awe,
Where nature[2] finds both honour, wealth and rest.
Our Christian freedom is, we have a law,
Which even the heathen think no power should wrest;

---

[1] 'The followers of Manes held that Christ came to save man from matter, and that his body was only a phantasm, as was his physical life on earth.' (Bullough).
[2] *nature:* human nature.

Yet proves it crooked as power lists[1] to draw,[2]
The rage or grace that lurks in princes' breasts.
   Opinion bodies may to shadows give,[3]
   But no burnt zone[4] it is, where people live.

XCI

Rewards of earth, nobility and fame,
To senses glory, and to conscience woe,
How little be you, for so great a name?
Yet less is he with men that thinks you so.
   For earthly power, that stands by fleshly wit,
   Hath banish'd that truth, which should govern it.

Nobility, power's golden fetter is,
Wherewith wise kings subjection do adorn,
To make man think her heavy yoke, a bliss,
Because it makes him more than he was born.
   Yet still a slave, dimm'd by mists of a crown,
   Lest he should see, what riseth, what pulls down.

Fame, that is but good words of evil deeds,
Begotten by the harm we have, or do,
Greatest far off, least ever where it breeds,
We both with dangers and disquiet woo.
   And in our flesh (the vanities' false glass)
   We thus deceiv'd adore these calves of brass.

XCII

Virgula divina, sorcerers call a rod,
Gather'd with vows, and magic sacrifice;
Which borne about, by influence doth nod,
Unto the silver, where it hidden lies;
   Which makes poor men to these black arts devout,
   Rich only in the wealth which hope finds out.

[1] *lists:* pleases.   [2] *to draw:* to pull (it) out of shape.
[3] *Opinion . . . give:* i.e. freedom, both for us and the Turks, is a shadow or illusion, but we think it is a real thing.   [4] *burnt zone:* i.e. a place inhospitable to life.

Nobility, this precious treasure is,
Laid up in secret mysteries of state,
Kings' creature, subjection's gilded bliss,
Where grace, not merit, seems to govern fate.
　　Mankind I think to be this rod divine,
　　For to the greatest ever they incline.

Eloquence, that is but wisdom speaking well,
(The poets feign) did make the savage tame;
Of ears and hearts chain'd unto tongues they tell;
I think nobility to be the same:
　　For be they fools, or speak they without wit,
　　We hold them wise, we fools bewonder it.

Invisible there is an art to go,
(They say that study Nature's secret works)
And art there is to make things greater show;
In nobleness I think this secret lurks,
　　For place a coronet on whom you will,
　　You straight see all great in him, but his ill.

XCIII

The Augurs were of all the world admir'd,
Flatter'd by consuls, honor'd by the State,
Because the event of all that was desir'd,
They seem'd to know, and keep the books of Fate:
　　Yet though abroad they thus did boast their wit,
　　Alone among themselves they scorned it.

Mankind, that with his wit doth gild his heart,
Strong in his passions, but in goodness weak;
Making great vices o'er the less an art,
Breeds wonder, and moves ignorance to speak,
　　Yet when his fame is to the highest borne,
　　We know enough to laugh his praise to scorn.

XCIV

Men, that delight to multiply desire,
Like tellers are that take coin but to pay,
Still tempted to be false, with little hire,
Black hands except, which they would have away:
    For, where power wisely audits her estate,
    The exchequer man's best recompense is hate.

The little maid that weareth out the day,
To gather flowers still covetous of more,
At night when she with her desire would play,
And let her pleasure wanton in her store,
    Discerns the first laid underneath the last,
    Wither'd, and so is all that we have pass'd:

Fix then on good desires, and if you find
Ambitious dreams or fears of overthwart,[1]
Changes, temptations, blooms of earthly mind,
Yet wave[2] not, since earth change, hath change of smart.[3]
    For lest man should think flesh a seat of bliss,
    God works that his joy mix'd with sorrow is.

XCV

Malice and love in their ways opposite,
The one to hurt itself for others' good;
The other, to have good by others' spite,
Both raging most, when they be most withstood;
    Though enemies, yet do in this agree,
    That both still break the hearts wherein they be.

[1] *overthwart:* contradiction, rebuff, opposition.   [2] *wave:* waver.
[3] This and the previous line are difficult. Ellis Fermor, in her edition, adopts the reading 'earthy' in l. 15, and emends l. 16 to 'Yet wave not, since earthy change hath change of smart.' Perhaps the best way of printing the line would be 'Yet wave not, since earth-change hath change of smart.' *of smart* painfully, in pain, with pain.

Malice a habit is, wrought in the spirit,
By intricate opinion's information;
Of scornful wrong or of suppressing merit,
Which either wounds men's states or reputation;
    And tyrant-like, though show of strength it bear,
    Yet is but weakness grown, enrag'd by fear.

Love is the true or false report of sense,
Who[1] sent as spies, returning news of worth,
With over-wonder breed the heart's offence,[2]
Not bringing in, but carrying pleasure forth,
    And child-like must have all things that they see,
    So much less lovers, than things loved be.[3]

Malice, like ruin, with itself overthrows
Mankind, and therefore plays a devil's part;
Love pulls itself down, but to build up those
It loves, and therefore bears an angel's heart.
    Tyrants through fear and malice feed on blood,
    Good kings secure at home, seek all men's good.

XCVI

In those years, when our sense, desire and wit,
Combine, that reason shall not rule the heart;
Pleasure is chosen as a goddess fit,
The wealth of Nature freely to impart;
Who like an idol doth apparel'd sit
In all the glories of opinion's art;
    The further off, the greater beauty showing,
    Lost only, or made less, by perfect knowing.

[1] *who:* refers to 'sense(s)'.

[2] *offence:* hurt, injury.

[3] *So much . . . loved be:* so much less do lovers love each other than they love things.

Which fair usurper runs a rebel's way,
10　For though elect of sense, wit and desire,
Yet rules she none, but such as will obey,
And to that end becomes what they aspire;
Making that torment, which before was play,
Those dews to kindle,[1] which did quench the fire:
　　Now honour's image, now again like lust,
　　But earthly still, and end repenting must.

While man, who satyr-like, then knows the flame,
When kissing of her fair-appearing light,
He feels a scorching power hid in the same,
20　Which cannot be revealed to the sight,
Yet doth by over-heat so shrink this frame,
Of fiery apparitions in delight;
　　That as in orbs,[2] where many passions reign,
　　What one affection joys, the rest complain.

In which confused sphere man being plac'd
With equal prospect over good or ill;
The one unknown, the other in distaste,[3]
Flesh, with her many molds of change and will,
So his affections carries on, and casts[4]
30　In declination[5] to the error still;
　　As by the truth he gets no other light,
　　But to see vice, a restless infinite.

---

[1] *Those dews to kindle:* i.e. making those dews into things that kindle.

[2] *orbs:* 'stars. He compares the joys of desire to the light of comets speedily burned out by their flames . . .' (Bullough).

[3] *the other in distaste:* i.e. the other being held in disgust or contempt.

[4] *carries on . . . casts:* I am not sure whether the potting image is continued or not in this line. The subject of both verbs is 'flesh'. The first part of the line could mean that flesh still continues or persists in man's affections; it could also, or instead, mean that flesh still carries man's affections imprinted on its many molds. Similarly, 'casts' could be intended in the sense of molding or of throwing, or in both. Greville is entirely capable of such puns, but the second is awkward because of the first two words of l. 30.

[5] *In declination:* in decline.

By which true map of his mortality,
Man's many idols are at once defaced,
And all hypocrisies of frail humanity,
Either exiled, waived, or disgraced;
Fall'n nature by the streams of vanity,
Forc'd up to call for grace above her placed:
    Whence from the depth of fatal desolation,
40   Springs up the height of his regeneration.

Which light of life doth all those shadows war
Of woe and lust, that dazzle and enthrall,
Whereby man's joys with goodness bounded are,
And to remorse his fears transformed all;
His six days labour past, and that clear star,
Figure of Sabbath's rest, rais'd by this fall;
    For God comes not till man be overthrown;
    Peace is the seed of grace, in dead flesh sown.

Flesh but the top, which only whips make go,
50   The steel whose rust is by afflictions worn,
The dust which good men from their feet must throw,
A living-dead thing, till it be new born,
A phoenix-life, that from self-ruin grows,
Or viper rather through her parents torn,
    A boat, to which the world itself is sea,
    Wherein the mind sails on her fatal way.

XCVII

Eternal Truth, almighty, infinite,
Only exiled from man's fleshly heart,
Where ignorance and disobedience fight,
In hell and sin, which shall have greatest part:
    When thy sweet mercy opens forth the light,
Of grace which giveth eyes unto the blind,
And with the Law even ploughest up our sprite
To faith, wherein flesh may salvation find;

Thou bidd'st us pray, and we do pray to thee,
But as to power and God without us plac'd,[1]
Thinking a wish may wear out vanity,
Or habits be by miracles defac'd.
  One thought to God we give, the rest to sin,
Quickly unbent is all desire of good,
True words pass out, but have no being within,
We pray to Christ, yet help to shed his blood;
  For while we say *Believe*, and feel it not,
Promise amends, and yet despair in it,
Hear Sodom judg'd, and go not out with Lot,
Make Law and Gospel riddles of the wit:
    We with the Jews even Christ still crucify,
    As[2] not yet come to our impiety.

XCVIII

Wrapp'd up, O Lord, in man's degeneration;
The glories of thy truth, thy joys eternal,
Reflect upon my soul dark desolation,
And ugly prospects o'er the sprites infernal.
    Lord, I have sinn'd, and mine iniquity,
    Deserves this hell; yet Lord deliver me.

Thy power and mercy never comprehended,
Rest lively-imag'd in my conscience wounded;
Mercy to grace, and power to fear extended,
Both infinite, and I in both confounded;
    Lord, I have sinn'd, and mine iniquity,
    Deserves this hell, yet lord deliver me.

[1] *But as . . . plac'd:* i.e. but as if we prayed to a power and God outside of us.
[2] *As:* 'who has' (Bullough).

If from this depth of sin, this hellish grave,
And fatal absence from my Saviour's glory,
I could implore his mercy, who can save,
And for my sins, not pains of sin, be sorry:
    Lord, from this horror of iniquity,
    And hellish grave, thou would'st deliver me.

XCIX

Down in the depth of mine iniquity,
That ugly centre of infernal spirits;
Where each sin feels her own deformity,
In those peculiar torments she inherits,
    Depriv'd of human graces, and divine,
    Even there appears this saving God of mine.

And in this fatal mirror of transgression,
Shows man as fruit of his degeneration,
The error's ugly infinite impression,[1]
Which bears the faithless down to desperation;
    Depriv'd of human graces and divine,
    Even there appears this saving God of mine.

In power and truth, almighty and eternal,
Which on the sin reflects strange desolation,
With glory scourging all the sprites infernal,
And uncreated hell with unprivation;
    Depriv'd of human graces, not divine,
    Even there appears this saving God of mine.

For on this sp'ritual cross condemned lying,
To pains infernal by eternal doom,
I see my Saviour for the same sins dying,
And from that hell I fear'd, to free me, come;
    Depriv'd of human graces, not divine,
    Thus hath his death rais'd up this soul of mine.

[1] *The error's . . . impression:* As Yvor Winters has pointed out, this line is the subject of the verb 'shows'.

C

In night when colours all to black are cast,
Distinction lost, or gone down with the light;
The eye a watch to inward senses plac'd,
Not seeing, yet still having power of sight,

Gives vain alarums to the inward sense,
Where fear stirr'd up with witty tyranny,[1]
Confounds all powers, and thorough self-offence,
Doth forge and raise impossibility:

Such as in thick depriving darknesses,
Proper reflections of the error be,
And images of self-confusednesses,
Which hurt imaginations only see;
    And from this nothing seen, tells news of devils,
    Which but expressions be of inward evils.

CI

Man's youth it is a field of large desires,
Which pleas'd within, doth all without them please,
For in this love of men live those sweet fires,
That kindle worth and kindness unto praise,
    And where self-love most from her selfness gives,
    Man greatest in himself, and others lives.

Old age again which deems this pleasure vain,
Dull'd with experience of unthankfulness,
Scornful of fame, as but effects of pain,[2]
Folds up that freedom in her narrowness,
    And for it only loves her own dreams best,
    Scorn'd and contemned is of all the rest.

[1] *witty tyranny:* i.e. the tyranny of what one imagines.
[2] *of pain:* i.e. of painful effort.

Such working youth there is again in state,
Which at the first with justice, piety,
Fame, and reward, true instruments of fate,
Strive to improve this frail humanity:
 By which as kings enlarge true worth in us,
 So crowns again are well enlarged thus.

But states grow old, when princes turn away
From honour, to take pleasure for their ends;
For that a large is, this a narrow way,
That wins a world, and this a few dark friends;
 The one improving worthiness spreads far,
 Under the other good things prisoners are.

Thus sceptres shadow-like, grow short or long,
As worthy, or unworthy princes reign,
And must contract, cannot be large or strong,
If man's weak humours real[1] power restrain,
 So that when power and nature[2] do oppose,
 All but the worst men are assur'd to lose.

For when respect, which is the strength of states,
Grows to decline by kings' descent within
That power's baby-creatures dare set rates[3]
Of scorn upon worth, honour upon sin;
 Then though kings, player-like, act glory's part,
 Yet all within them is but fear and art.

[1] *real:* i.e. as opposed to 'shadow-like'.
[2] *nature:* human nature.
[3] *rates:* taxes.

CII

The serpent, Sin, by showing human lust
Visions and dreams enticed man to do
Follies, in which exceed his God he must,
And know more than he was created to,
 A charm which made the ugly sin seem good,
 And is by fall'n spirits only understood.

Now man no sooner from his mean creation,[1]
Trod this excess of uncreated sin,
But straight he chang'd his being to privation,
10 Horror and death at this gate passing in;
 Whereby immortal life, made for man's good,
 Is since become the hell of flesh and blood.

But grant that there were no eternity,
That life were all, and pleasure life of it,
In sin's excess there yet confusions be,
Which spoil his peace, and passionate[2] his wit,
 Making his nature less, his reason thrall,
 To tyranny of vice unnatural.

And as hell-fires, not wanting heat, want light;
20 So these strange witchcrafts, which like pleasure be,
Not wanting fair enticements, want delight,
Inward being nothing but deformity;
 And do at open doors let frail powers in
 To that strait building,[3] Little-ease[4] of sin.

---

[1] *mean creation:* 'primal state intermediate between God and privation'. (Bullough).

[2] *passionate:* impassion.

[3] *strait building:* an alternative reading is 'strait-binding'.

[4] *Little-ease:* 'a narrow place of confinement; spec. the name of a dungeon in the Tower of London'. (O.E.D.) See Introduction (p. 31).

Yet is there aught more wonderful than this?
That man, even in the state of his perfection,
All things uncurs'd, nothing yet done amiss,
And so in him no base of his defection;
 Should fall from God, and break his Maker's will,
30 Which could have no end, but to know the ill.

I ask the rather since in Paradise,
Eternity was object to[1] his passion,
And he in goodness like his Maker wise,
As from his spirit taking life and fashion;
 What greater power there was to master this,
 Or how a less could work, my question is?

For who made all, 'tis sure yet could not make,
Any above himself, as princes can,[2]
So as, against his will no power could take,
40 A creature from him; nor corrupt a man;
 And yet who thinks he marr'd, that made us good,
 As well may think God less than flesh and blood.

Where did our being then seek out privation?
Above, within, without us all was pure,
Only the angels[3] from their discreation,
By smart[4] declar'd no being was secure,
 But that transcendent goodness which subsists,
 By forming and reforming what it lists.

So as within the man there was no more,
50 But possibility to work upon,
And in these spirits, which were fall'n before,
An abstract curs'd eternity alone;
 Refin'd by their high places in creation,
 To add more craft and malice to temptation.

[1] *object to:* object of.
[2] *as princes can:* i.e. because some princes can elect an emperor.
[3] *the angels:* i.e. the fallen angels.   [4] *smart:* suffering.

Now with what force upon these middle spheres,
Of probable, and possibility,
Which no one constant demonstration bears,
And so can neither bind, nor bounded be;
    What those could work, that having lost their God,
60   Aspire to be our tempters and our rod,

Too well is witness'd by this fall of ours,
For we not knowing yet that there was ill,
Gave easy credit to deceiving powers,
Who wrought upon us only by our will;
    Persuading, like it, all was to it free,
    Since where no sin was, there no law could be.

And as all finite things seek infinite,
From thence deriving what beyond them is;
So man was led by charms of this dark sp'rit,
70   Which he could not know till he did amiss;
    To trust those serpents, who learn'd since they fell,
    Knew more than we did; even their own-made hell.

Which crafty odds made us those clouds embrace,
Where sin in ambush lay to overthrow
Nature,[1] (that would presume to fathom grace)
Or could believe what God said was not so:
    Sin, then we know thee not, and could not hate,
    And now we know thee, now it is too late.

CIII

O false and treacherous probability,[2]
Enemy of truth, and friend to wickedness;
With whose blear eyes opinion learns to see
Truth's feeble party here, and barrenness.

[1] *Nature:* human nature.
[2] *probability:* 'That which on present evidence and thought seems likely to be true. Greville means the sphere of metaphysical enquiry in which human reason tries to solve eternal problems; cf. LXXXVIII' (Bullough).

When thou hast thus misled humanity,
And lost obedience in the pride of wit,
With reason dar'st thou judge the deity,
And in thy flesh make bold to fashion it.

Vain thought, the Word of power a riddle is,
And till the veils be rent, the flesh new-born,
Reveals no wonders of that inward bliss,
Which but[1] where faith is, everywhere finds scorn;
   Who therefore censures God with fleshly sprite,
   As well in time may wrap up[2] infinite.

CIV

Two sects there be in this world opposite,
The one make Mahomet a deity,
A tyrant Tartar rais'd by war and sleight,
Ambitious ways of infidelity:
   The world their heaven is, the world is great,
   And racketh those hearts, where it hath receipt.[3]

The other sect of cloister'd people is,
Less to the world, with which they seem to war,
And so in less things drawn to do amiss,
As all lusts, less than lust of conquest are:
   Now if of God, both those have but the name,
   What mortal idol then, can equal Fame?[4]

[1] *but:* except.

[2] *wrap up:* 'to involve or enfold (a subject or matter) so as to obscure or disguise the true or full nature of it' (O.E.D.).

[3] *where it hath receipt:* i.e. where it is (totally) accepted.

[4] *Fame:* monks too seek glory on earth, presumably by 'seeming to war' with the world and achieving an apparent conquest.

CV

Three things there be in man's opinion dear,
Fame, many friends, and Fortune's dignities:
False visions all, which in our sense appear,
To sanctify desire's idolatries.

For what is Fortune, but a wat'ry glass?
Whose crystal forehead wants a steely back,
Where rain and storms bear all away that was,
Whose shape alike both depths and shallows wrack.

Fame again, which from blinding power takes light,
Both Caesar's shadow is,[1] and Cato's friend,
The child of humour, not allied to right,
Living by oft exchange of winged end.[2]

And many friends, false strength of feeble mind,
Betraying equals, as true slaves to might;
Like echoes still send voices down the wind,
But never in adversity find right.

Then man, though virtue of extremities,
The middle be,[3] and so hath two to one,
By place and nature constant enemies,
And against both these no strength but her own,
    Yet quit thou for her,[4] friends, fame, Fortune's throne;
    Devils, there many be, and Gods but one.

[1] *Caesar's shadow is:* because 'Caesar was ambitious'.
[2] *winged end:* Is this a circumlocution for 'arrow'? (O.E.D. says 'end' could
mean 'the point of a spear', but gives no example later than the year 1400.)
[3] *though virtue of extremities, The middle be:* though virtue lies between extremes.
[4] *her:* i.e. virtue's.

CVI

How falls it out, the sincere magistrate,[1]
(Who keeps the course of justice sacredly)
Reaps from the people reverence, and hate,
But not the love which follows liberty?

The cause is plain, since tax on people's good[2]
Is hardly borne, sense[3] having no foresight,
Hates reason's works as strange to flesh and blood,
Whence he that strives to keep man's heart upright

Taxes his fancies[4] at an higher rate;
And laying laws upon his frailty,
Brings all his vices to a bankrupt state,
So much is true worth more refin'd than we:
    Again, who tasks men's wealth, pierce but their skin,
    Who roots their vice out, must pierce deeper in.

CVII

Isis, in whom the poet's feigning wit,
Figures the Goddess of Authority,
And makes her on an ass in triumph sit,
As if power's throne were man's humility;
Inspire this ass, as well becoming it,
Even like a type of wind-blown vanity:
    With pride to bear power's gilding scorching heat
    For no hire, but opinion to be great.

[1] *magistrate:* ruler.   [2] *good:* goods.
[3] *sense:* the senses.   [4] *fancies:* i.e. products of the senses.

So as this beast, forgetting what he bears,
Bridled and burden'd by the hand of might,
While he beholds the swarms of hope and fears,
Which wait upon ambition infinite,
Proud of the glorious furniture he wears,
Takes all to Isis offer'd, but[1] his right;
    Till weariness, the spur, or want of food,
    Makes gilded curbs of all beasts understood.

CVIII

What is the cause, why states, that war and win,
Have honour, and breed men of better fame,
Than states in peace, since war and conquest sin
In blood, wrong liberty, all trades of shame?
    Force-framing instruments, which it must use,
    Proud in excess and glory to abuse.

The reason is; peace is a quiet nurse
Of idleness, and idleness the field,
Where wit and power change all seeds to the worse,
By narrow self-will upon which they build,
    And thence bring forth captiv'd inconstant ends,
    Neither to princes, nor to people friends.

Besides, the sins of peace on subjects feed,
And thence wound power, which for it all things can,
With wrong to one despairs in many breed,
For while laws' oaths, power's creditors to man,
    Make humble subjects dream of native right,
    Man's faith abus'd adds courage to despite.

Where conquest works by strength, and stirs up fame,
A glorious echo, pleasing doom of pain,
    Which in the sleep of death yet keeps a name,
    And makes detracting loss speak ill in vain.

[1] *but:* except.

For to great actions time so friendly is,
As o'er the means (albeit the means be ill)
It casts forgetfulness; veils things amiss,
With power and honour to encourage will.

Besides things hard a reputation bear,
To die resolv'd though guilty wonder breeds,
Yet what strength those be[1] which can blot out fear,
And to self-ruin joyfully proceeds,
    Ask them that from the ashes of this fire,
    With new lives still to such new flames aspire.[2]

CIX

Sion lies waste, and thy Jerusalem,
O Lord, is fall'n to utter desolation,
Against thy prophets, and thy holy men,
The sin hath wrought a fatal combination,
    Profan'd thy name, thy worship overthrown,
    And made thee living Lord, a God unknown.

Thy powerful laws, thy wonders of creation,
Thy Word incarnate, glorious heaven, dark hell,
Lie shadowed under man's degeneration,
Thy Christ still crucifi'd for doing well,
    Impiety, O Lord, sits on thy throne,
    Which makes thee living light, a God unknown.

Man's superstition hath thy truths entomb'd,
His atheism again her pomps defaceth,
That sensual unsatiable vast womb
Of thy seen Church, thy unseen Church disgraceth;
    There lives no truth with them that seem thine own,
    Which makes thee living Lord, a God unknown.

[1] *those be:* 'in them there is' (Bullough).

[2] *Ask them . . . flames aspire:* 'No soldier comes back (like the Phoenix) from
the dead to seek a similar death in battle again. Hence we cannot know whether his
martial courage is true strength (and acceptable to God). Obviously Greville feels
that it is not.' (Bullough).

Yet unto thee, Lord, (mirror of transgression)
We, who for earthly idols, have forsaken
Thy heavenly image (sinless pure impression)
And so in nets of vanity lie taken,
    All desolate implore that to thine own,
    Lord, thou no longer live a God unknown.

Yet Lord let Israel's plagues not be eternal,
Nor sin for ever cloud thy sacred mountains,
Nor with false flames spiritual but infernal,
Dry up thy mercy's ever-springing fountains,
    Rather, sweet Jesus, fill up time and come,
    To yield the sin her everlasting doom.

Selected Choruses
from the Plays

From *Mustapha*
CHORUS TERTIUS
OF TIME: ETERNITY

TIME

What mean these mortal children of mine own,
Ungratefully, against me to complain,
That all I build is by me overthrown?
Vices put under to rise up again?
    That on my wheels both good and ill do move,
    The one beneath, while th'other is above?

Day, night, hours, arts, all God or men create,
The world doth charge me, that I restless change;
Suffer no being in a constant state:
10 Alas! Why are my revolutions strange
    Unto these natures, made to fall, or climb,
    With that sweet genius, ever-moving Time?

What weariness; what loathsome desolations
Would plague these life- and death-begetting creatures?
Nay what absurdity in my creations
Were it, if Time-born had eternal features;
    This nether orb, which is corruption's sphere,[1]
    Not being able long one shape to bear.

Could pleasure live? Could worth have reverence?
20 Laws, arts, or sects (mere probabilities)[2]
Keep up their reputation in man's sense,
If novelty did not renew his eyes;
    Or Time take mildly from him what he knew,
    Making both me, and mine, to each still new?

[1] *orb . . . sphere:* i.e. the earth. 'The different spheres of heaven in the old astronomy were each moved and directed by an Intelligence or Angel.' H. J. C. Grierson, *Metaphysical Lyrics and Poems of the Seventeenth Century*, 1921, p. 228. The Angel of earth, then, is corruption.   [2] *probabilities:* see note [2] p. 133.

Daughter of Heaven am I; but[1] God, none greater;
Pure like my parents; life, and death of action;
Author of ill success to every creature,
Whose pride against my periods makes a faction:
  With me who go along, rise while they be;
30   Nothing of mine respects Eternity.

Kings! why do you then blame me, whom I choose,
As my anointed, from the potter's ore;[2]
And to advance you made the people lose,
While you to me acknowledged your power?
  Be confident all thrones subsist in me:
  I am the measure of felicity.

Mahomet in vain, one trophy of my might,
Rais'd by my chang'd aspect to other nations,
Strives to make his succession infinite,
40 And rob my wheels of growth, state, declination.
  But he, and all else that would master Time,
  In mortal spheres, shall find my power sublime.

I bring the truth to light; detect the ill;
My native greatness scorneth bounded ways;
Untimely power a few days ruin will;
Yea, worth itself falls, till I list to raise.
  The earth is mine: of earthly things the care
  I leave to men, that like them, earthly are.

Ripe I yet am not to destroy succession;
50 The vice of other kingdoms give[3] him Time.
The Fates, without me, can make no progression;
By me alone, even truth can fall, or climb:
  The instant petty webs, without me[4] spun,
  Untimely ended be, as they begun.

---

[1] *but:* but for.
[2] *As my ... ore:* refers to Agathocles of Syracuse, raised from potter to king.
ore: clay.
[3] *give:* 'gives' (Bullough).   [4] *without me:* without taking account of me.

[144]

Not kings, but I, can Nemesis send forth,
The judgments of revenge, and wrong, are mine:
My stamps alone do warrant real worth;
How do untimely virtues else decline?
    For son, or father, to destroy each other,
60   Are bastard deeds, where Time is not the mother.

Such is the work this state hath undertaken,
And keeps in clouds; with purpose to advance
False counsels; in their self-craft justly shaken,
As grounded on my slave and shadow Chance.
    Nay more; my child Occasion is not free
    To bring forth good, or evil, without me.

And shall I for revealing this misdeed,
By tying future to the present ill,
Which keeps disorder's ways from happy speed,
70   Be guilty made of man's still-erring will?
    Shall I, that in myself still golden am,
    By their gross metal, bear an iron name?

No; let man draw, by his own cursed square,
Such crooked lines, as his frail thoughts affect:[1]
And, like things that of nothing framed are,
Decline unto that centre of defect:
    I will disclaim his downfall, and stand free,
    As native rival to Eternity.

ETERNITY

    What means this new-born child of planets' motion?
80   This finite elf of man's vain acts, and errors?
    Whose changing wheels in all thoughts stir commotion?
    And in her own face, only, bears the mirror.
        A mirror in which, since Time took her fall,
        Mankind sees ill increase; no good at all.

            [1] *affect:* aspire to.
K   [145]

Because in your vast mouth you hold your tail,
As coupling ages past with times to come:
Do you presume your trophies shall not fail,
As both creation's cradle, and her tomb?
    Or for[1] beyond yourself you cannot see,
90   By days, and hours, would you eternal be?

Time is the weakest work of my creation,
And, if not still repair'd, must straight decay:
The mortal take not my true constellation,[2]
And so are dazzled, by her nimble sway,
    To think her course long; which if measur'd right,
    Is but a minute of my infinite.

A minute which doth her subsistence tie;
Subsistences which, in not being, be:
Shall is to come; and *Was* is passed by;
100 Time present cements this duplicity:
    And if one must, of force, be like the other,
    Of Nothing is not Nothing made the mother?

Why strives Time then to parallel with me?
What be her types of longest lasting glory?
Arts, mitres, laws, moments, supremacy,[3]
Of Nature's erring alchemy the story:
    From Nothing sprang this point, and must, by course,
    To that confusion turn again, or worse.

For she, and all her mortal offsprings, built
110 Upon the moving base of self-conceit;
Which constant form can neither take, nor yield;
But still change shapes, to multiply deceit;:
    Like playing atomi, in vain contending,
    Though they beginning had, to have no ending.

[1] *for:* because.
[2] *my true constellation:* 'Mortals do not find the true position of the stars in the constellation which I dominate.' (Bullough).
[3] *moments, supremacy:* I suggest emending the phrase to 'momen ts' supremacy'.

[146]

I, that at once see Time's distinct progression;
I, in whose bosom *Was*, and *Shall*, still be;
I, that in causes work th' effect's succession,
Giving both good, and ill, their destiny;
    Thought I bind all, yet can receive no bound;
120   But see the finite still itself confound.

Time! therefore know thy limits, and strive not
To make thyself, or thy works infinite,
Whose essence only is to write, and blot:
Thy changes prove thou has no 'stablish'd right.
    Govern thy mortal sphere, deal not with mine:
    Time but the servant is of Power Divine.

Blame thou this present state, that will blame thee;
Brick-wall[1] your errors from one, to another;
Both fail alike unto Eternity,
130 Goodness of no mix'd course can be the mother.
    Both you and yours do covet states eternal;
    Whence, though pride end, your pains yet be infernal.

Ruin this mass; work change in all estates,
Which, when they serve not me, are in your power:
Give unto their corruption dooms of Fate;
Let your vast womb your Cadmus-men devour.
    The vice yields scope enough for you, and hell,
    To compass ill ends by not doing well.

Let Mustapha[2] by your course be destroy'd,
140 Let your wheels, made to wind up, and untwine,
Leave nothing constantly to be enjoy'd:
For your scythe mortal must to harm incline,
    Which, as this world, your maker, doth grow old,
    Dooms her, for your toys, to be bought, and sold.

[1] *Brick-wall:* (corruption of the French 'bricoler') cause to rebound.
[2] *Mustapha:* in the play where this chorus comes.

Cross your own steps; hasten to make, and mar;
With your vicissitudes please, displease your own:
Your three light wheels[1] of sundry fashions are,
And each, by others' motion, overthrown.
　　Do what you can: mine shall subsist by me:
150　I am the measure of felicity.

From *Mustapha*
CHORUS QUINTUS
TARTARORUM ·

Vain superstition![2] Glorious style[3] of weakness!
Sprung from the deep disquiet of man's passion,
To desolation, and despair of Nature:
Thy texts bring princes' titles into question:
Thy prophets set on work the sword of tyrants:
They manacle sweet truth with their distinctions:
Let virtue blood: teach cruelty for God's sake;
Fashioning one God; yet him of many fashions,
Like many-headed error, in their passions.
　　Mankind! Trust not these superstitious dreams,
Fear's idols, pleasure's relics, sorrow's pleasures.
They make the wilful hearts their holy temples:
The rebels unto government their martyrs,
　　No: thou child of false miracles begotten!
False miracles, which are but ignorance of cause,
Lift up the hopes of thy abjected prophets:
Courage, and worth abjure thy painted heavens.
Sickness, thy blessings are; misery, thy trial;
Nothing, thy way unto eternal being;
Death, to salvation; and the grave to Heaven.
So blest be they, so angel'd, so eterniz'd

[1] *three light wheels:* past, present, and future, I suppose.
[2] *superstition:* i.e. specifically Mohammedanism.
[3] *style:* title.

[148]

That tie their senses to thy senseless glories,
And die, to cloy the after-age with stories.
   Man should make much of life, as Nature's table,[1]
Wherein she writes the cypher of her glory.
Forsake not Nature, nor misunderstand her:
Her mysteries are read without faith's eyesight:
She speaketh in our flesh; and from our senses,
Delivers down her wisdoms to our reason.
If any man would break her laws to kill,
Nature doth, for defence, allow offences.
She neither taught the father to destroy:
Nor promis'd any man, by dying, joy.

From *Mustapha*
CHORUS SACERDOTUM

Oh wearisome condition of humanity!
Born under one law, to another bound:
Vainly begot, and yet forbidden vanity,
Created sick, commanded to be sound:
What meaneth Nature by these diverse laws?
Passion and reason, self-division cause:
Is it the mark, or majesty of power
To make offences that it may forgive?
Nature herself, doth her own self deflower,
To hate those errors she herself doth give.
For how should man think that, he may not do
If Nature did not fail, and punish too?
Tyrant to others, to herself unjust,
Only commands things difficult and hard.
Forbids us all things, which it knows is lust,
Makes easy pains, unpossible reward.
If Nature did not take delight in blood,

[1] *table:* book.
[149]

She would have made more easy ways to good.
We that are bound by vows, and by promotion,
With pomp of holy sacrifice and rites,
To teach belief in good and still devotion,
To preach of Heaven's wonders, and delights:
Yet when each of us, in his own heart looks,
He finds the God there, far unlike his books.

From *Alaham*
PROLOGUS

The speech of a Ghost, one of the old Kings of Ormus.

Thou monster horrible! under whose ugly doom,
Down in eternity's perpetual night,
Man's temporal sins bear torments infinite:
For change of desolation, must I come
To tempt the earth, and to profane the light;
From mournful silence, where pain dares not roar
With liberty; to multiply it more?
Nor from the loathsome puddle Acheron,
Made foul with common sins, whose filthy damps
10 Feed Lethe's sink, forgetting all but moan:
Nor from that foul infernal shadowed lamp,
Which lighted Sisiphus to roll his stone:
These be but bodies' plagues, the skirts of hell;
I come from whence death's seat doth death excel.
A place there is upon no centre placed,
Deep under depths, as far as is the sky
Above the earth; dark, infinitely spaced:
Pluto the king, the kingdom misery.
The crystal[1] may God's glorious seat resemble;

[1] *crystal:* i.e. a crystal in its brightness and clarity bears a weak resemblance to heaven, but the greatest horror we can know on earth bears no comparison to those of hell.

20 Horror itself these horrors but dissemble.
        Privation would reign there, by God not made;
    But creature of uncreated sin,
    Whose being is all beings to invade,
    To have no ending though it did begin:
    And so of past, things present, and to come,
    To give depriving, not tormenting doom,
    But horror, in the understanding mix'd;
    And memory, by eternity's seal wrought;
    Unto the bodies of the evil fix'd,
30 And into reason by our passion brought,
    Here rack'd, torn, and exil'd from unity;
    Though come from nothing, must for ever be.
        The sins that enter here are capital:
    Atheism, where creatures their Creator lose;
    Unthankful Pride, Nature and grace's fall;
    Hate of mankind, in man unnatural;
    Hypocrites, which bodies leave, and shadows choose,
    The persons, either kings by fortune blest,
    Or men by Nature made kings of the rest.
40 Here tyrants that corrupt authority,
    Counsel'd out of the fears of wickedness,
    Cunning in mischief, proud in cruelty,
    Are furies made, to plague the weaker ghosts,
    Whose souls, enticing pleasure only lost.
    The weaker kings, whose more unconstant vice
    Their states unto their humours made a prey;
    For suffering more-than-kings[1] to tyrannize,
    Are damn'd; though here to be, yet not to stay:
    For back they go, to tempt with every sin,
50 As easiest it the world may enter in.
        Myself sometimes was such; Ormus my state.
    I bare the name; yet did my basshas[2] reign:
    Trusts to few windows[3] are unfortunate;

[1] *more-than-kings:* for example the basshas in l. 52.
[2] *basshas:* grandees.
[3] *windows:* the image is odd: it appears to mean 'outlets of power'.

For subjects' growing full is princes' wane.
Lo; all misdeeds procure their own misfate;
For by my trusted basshas was I slain:
Now sent to tear down my posterity,
That have their sin's inheritance from me.
   My first charge is, the ruin of mine own,
60 Hell keeping knowledge still of earthliness,
None coming there but spirits overgrown,
And more embodied into wickedness:
The body by the spirit living ever;
The spirit in the body joying never:
In Heaven perchance no such affections be;
Those angel-souls in flesh imprisoned,
Like strangers living in mortality,
Still more, and more, themselves enspirited,
Refining Nature to eternity;
70 By being maids in earth's adulterous bed:
And idly forget all here below,
Where we our parents,[1] but to plague them, know.
   My next charge is, from this dark regiment[2]
With wiles to scourge this age effeminate;
Not open force, or humours violent:
Time fashions minds, minds manners, manners fate.
Here rage gives place, wit must rule ill-intent.
Proud honour being an ill for this state
Too strong; sleight must mislead the innocent;
80 Craft, the corrupt. For though none dare be just,
Yet coward ill, with care, grow wicked must. . . .

---

[1] *parents:* relatives.   [2] *regiment:* i.e. place ruled over.

From *Alaham*
CHORUS QUARTUS
OF PEOPLE

Like as strong winds do work upon the sea,
Stirring, and tossing waves to war each other:
So princes do with peoples' humours play,
As if confusion were the sceptre's mother.
　　But crowns! take heed: when humble things mount high,
　　The winds oft calm before those billows lie.

When we are all wrong'd, had we all one mind,
Whom could you punish? what could you reserve?
Again, as hope, and fear distract mankind,
Knew kings their strength, our freedom were to serve.
　　But Fate doth to herself reserve both these,[1]
　　With each to punish other, when it please.

Grant that we be the stuff for princes' art,
By, and on it, to build their thrones above us:
Yet if kings be the head, we be the heart;
And know we love no soul, that doth not love us.
　　Men's many passions judge the worst at length,
　　And they that do so, easily know their strength:

With bruit, and rumour, as with hope, and fear,
You lay us low, or lift us from our earth;
You try what nature, what our states[2] can bear;
By law you bind the liberties of birth;
　　Making the people bellows unto fame,
　　Which ushers heavy dooms with evil name.

[1] *these:* hope and fear.
[2] *what nature, what our states:* what our natures and what our property.

[153]

Kings govern people, over-rack them not:
Fleece us; but do not clip us to the quick.
Think not with good, and ill, to write, and blot:
The good doth vanish, where the ill doth stick.
 Hope not with trifles to grow popular;
30 Wounds that are heal'd for ever leave a scar.

To offer people shows makes us too great:
Princes descend not, keep yourselves above.
The sun draws not our brows up, but our sweat:[1]
Your safest rack to wind us up is love.
 To mask your vice in pomps is vainly done:
 Motes lie not hidden in beams of a sun.

The stamp of sovereignty makes current
Home-brass to buy, or sell, as well as gold:
Yet mark! the people's standard is the warrant
40 What man ought not to do, and what he should.
 Of words we are the grammar, and of deeds
 The harvest both is ours, and eke the seeds.

We are the glass of power, and do reflect
That image back, which it to us presents:
If princes flatter, straight we do neglect;
If they be fine,[2] we see, yet seem content.
 Nor can the throne, which monarchs do live in,
 Shadow kings' faults, or sanctify their sin.

Make not the Church to us an instrument
50 Of bondage, to yourselves of liberty:
Obedience there confirms your government;
Our sovereigns, God's subalterns you be:
 Else while kings fashion God in human light,
 Men see, and scorn what is not infinite.

[1] *The sun . . . our sweat:* 'Be like the sun, which in shining upon us from a distance does not make us raise our eyebrows (as in supercilious pride) but makes us perspire (as by labour)' (Bullough).
[2] *fine:* fastidious.

Make not the end of justice, chequer-gain,[1]
It is the liberality of kings:
Oppression, and extortion ever reign,
When laws look more on sceptres, than on things.
 Make crooked that line which you measure by;
60 And mar the fashion straight of monarchy.

Why do you[2] then profane your royal line,
Which we hold sacred, and dare not approach?
Their wounds, and wrongs prove you are not divine,
And we learn, by example, to encroach.
 Your father's loss of eyes foretells his end:
 By craft, which lets down princes, we ascend.

How shall the people hope? how stay their fear,
When old foundations daily are made new?
Uncertain is a heavy load to bear;
70 What is not constant sure was never true.
 Excess in one makes all indefinite:
 Where nothing is our own, there what delight?

Kings then take heed! Men are the books of fate,
Wherein your vices deep engraven lie,
To show our God the grief of every state.
And though great bodies do not straightways die;
 Yet know, your errors have this proper doom,
 Even in our ruin to prepare your tomb.

   [1] *chequer:* exchequer.   [2] *you:* Alaham.

Index of First Lines

[156]

Down in the depth of mine iniquity, 128

Eternal Truth, almighty, infinite, 126
Eyes, why did you bring unto me those graces, 48

Faction, that ever dwells, 63
Fair dog, which so my heart dost tear asunder, 46
Farewell sweet boy, complain not of my truth, 117
Fie foolish earth, think you the heaven wants glory, 55
Fortune, art thou not forc'd sometimes to scorn, 108

Goodfellows whom men commonly do call, 65

Heavens! see how bringing-up corrupts or betters, 65
How falls it out, the sincere magistrate, 136

I offer wrong to my beloved saint, 56
I with whose colours Myra dress'd her head, 58
In night when colours all to black are cast, 129
In the time when herbs and flowers, 101
In the window o f a grange, 99
In those years, when our sense, desire and wit, 124
Isis, in whom the poet's feigning wit, 136

Juno, that on her head love's livery carried, 52

Kings that in youth like all things else, are fine, 68

Light rage and grief, limbs of unperfect love, 82
Like as strong winds do work upon the sea, 153
Love, I did send you forth enamell'd fair, 97
Love is the peace, whereto all thoughts do strive, 118
Love, of man's wandering thoughts the restless being, 51
Love, the delight of all well-thinking minds, 45

Malice and love in their ways opposite, 123
Man, dream no more of curious mysteries, 119

[157]

The world, that all contains, is ever moving, 49
Three things there be in man's opinion dear, 135
Thou monster horrible! under whose ugly doom, 150
Two sects there be in this world opposite, 134

Unconstant thoughts where light desires do move, 95
Under a throne I saw a virgin sit, 113

Vain superstition! glorious style of weakness, 148
Virgula divina, sorcerers call a rod, 121

Was ever man so overmatch'd with boy, 61
What is the cause, why states, that war and win, 137
What mean these mortal children of mine own, 143
When all this All doth pass from age to age, 96
When as man's life, the light of human lust, 119
When gentle beauty's over-wanton kindness, 54
While that my heart an altar I did make, 95
Who grace, for zenith had, from whom no shadows grow, 113
Who trusts for trust, or hopes of love for love, 47
Who worships Cupid, doth adore a boy, 90
Whoever sails near to Bermuda coast, 87
Why how now Cupid, do you covet change, 57
Why how now reason, how are you amazed, 53
Wrapp'd up, O Lord, in man's degeneration, 127

You faithless boy, persuade you me to reason, 62
You little stars that live in skies, 47
You that seek what life is in death, 113

Selected Poems of Fulke Greville

Books by Thom Gunn

*

FIGHTING TERMS
THE SENSE OF MOVEMENT
MY SAD CAPTAINS
TOUCH

*

SELECTED POEMS
(in one volume with Ted Hughes)